OXFORD
UNIVERSITY PRESS

Ben Wetz

Diana Pye

English Plus

Student's Book 4

◻◻◻◻◻◻◻◻ CONTENTS

Starter unit

1 🔊 1.02 Complete phrases 1–10 with the verbs in the box. Then listen and check.

> do   go   send   download   pass   get
> get up   ~~spend~~   earn   stay   watch

spend time
1 ___ text messages
2 ___ bored
3 ___ exercise
4 ___ late
5 ___ music from the internet
6 ___ TV
7 ___ at home
8 ___ exams
9 ___ online
10 ___ money

2 Complete the sentences with phrases in exercise 1.

1 I like surfing the internet. I ___ every day.
2 I often ___ and listen to it on my mp3 player.
3 Sally always carries her mobile phone so that she can ___ to her friends. She's sending one now!
4 Tim doesn't ___ at the weekend. He plays football on Saturday mornings.
5 Rob needs to ___ some ___. He isn't very fit!
6 Do you ___ when you're on your own? Or do you have some interesting hobbies?
7 I'm doing my homework at the moment. I want to ___ my ___.

3 🔊 1.03 Listen to Liza and Sam doing the *Your lifestyle* questionnaire. Who likes studying, Liza or Sam?

4 **ACTIVATE** Do the *Your lifestyle* questionnaire with a partner. How similar or different are your lifestyles? Who has got a more active lifestyle?

> How much time do you spend doing exercise each day?

> About forty minutes. I usually walk to and from school.

> I don't do much exercise on weekdays, but I go swimming on Saturdays.

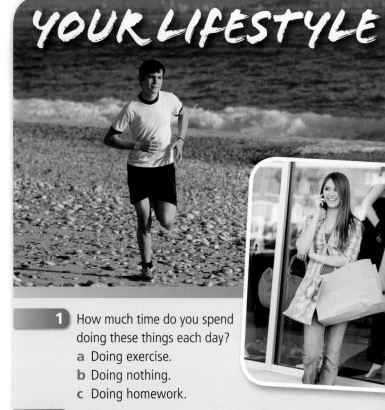

YOUR LIFESTYLE

1 How much time do you spend doing these things each day?
a Doing exercise.
b Doing nothing.
c Doing homework.

2 Which of these activities do you enjoy most?
a Going shopping.   b Watching TV.
c Doing sport.

3 How do you spend your time on Saturdays? Choose the statement which is most true for you.
a I usually stay at home with my family.
b I get up late and then I watch TV.
c I usually do sport.

4 How often do you ...
a send text messages?   b read a book?
c go swimming?

5 When you get bored, what do you usually do?
a I watch TV.   b I have something to eat.
c I go online.

6 Do you ever make dinner for your family?
a No, never. I hate cooking.
b Yes, sometimes.
c I sometimes make a meal, but only for me.

7 Which of these things do you dislike most?
a Tidying my room.   b Getting up early.
c Doing nothing.

8 Which of these things is most important in your life?
a Passing exams.
b Earning money.
c Having fun.

LANGUAGE FOCUS ■ Present tenses • Verbs + -ing / to
I can talk about my interests.

Present simple and continuous

1 Complete the sentences from exercise 2 on page 4. Then answer questions a–c.

1 She's ___ one now!
2 Tim ___ get up late at the weekend.
3 I ___ my homework at the moment.
4 I ___ online every day.

a Which sentences are present simple and which are present continuous?
b Which sentences refer to actions happening now?
c Which sentences refer to repeated actions or routines?

(More practice ⇨ Workbook page 5)

2 Complete the email using the correct form of the verbs in brackets.

To: Phil
From: Kathy

Hi Phil

How are things? **Are you enjoying** (you / enjoy) your holiday? ¹___ (you / like) Spain? I ²___ (have) a fantastic time here in Greece. We ³___ (not stay) in a flat, we decided to camp this year instead. It's much more fun. Every morning, I ⁴___ (go) swimming very early. I enjoy being on my own on the beach. Most people ⁵___ (not come) until later. Of course, my brother Scott ⁶___ (not swim) with me. He never ⁷___ (get up) before lunchtime!

I must go now. Dad ⁸___ (call) me. He ⁹___ (cook) dinner on the barbecue and I think it's ready.

Kathy

3 Write questions for 1–6. Then look at the email and ask and answer the questions with a partner.

Kathy / have a good holiday?
Is Kathy having a good holiday?

1 Kathy's family / stay in a flat?
2 Kathy / like camping?
3 when / Kathy / go swimming?
4 what / Scott / do in the morning?
5 Kathy's dad / cook lunch?
6 they / have a barbecue?

(Is Kathy having a good holiday?)

(Yes, she's having a fantastic time.)

Verbs + -ing / to

4 Match the sentence halves. Which verbs are followed by *to* and which are followed by *-ing*?

1 I'm really tired. I need …
2 I enjoy sport, but I hate …
3 I'm quite lazy. I can't stand …
4 I'm into maths. I don't mind …
5 I need to pass my exams. I want …
6 I like watching DVDs and I love …
7 I'm into cooking. I enjoy …
8 I'm having a great time. I don't want …

a going to the cinema.
b to be a lawyer when I'm older.
c doing algebra.
d tidying my room.
e to go home yet.
f playing basketball.
g to go to bed early.
h making dinner for my family.

(More practice ⇨ Workbook page 5)

5 Complete the sentences with your own ideas.

1 I like …   5 I need …
2 I love …   6 I don't mind …
3 I hate …   7 I don't want …
4 I enjoy …   8 I'm into …

6 **ACTIVATE** Study the key phrases. Then interview people in your class and find someone with the same interests as you. Use the key phrases, the words in the box and your own ideas.

KEY PHRASES ◯ Talking about your interests

Do you like / enjoy … -ing?	Yes, I (really) love it.
Are you into … -ing?	It's OK. / I don't mind it.
	No, I (really) hate it.

read   get up late   play video games
go online   watch TV   do exercise

(Are you into doing exercise?)   (No, I hate it.)

◯ Finished?
Write sentences about things your partner likes or doesn't like doing.
He likes playing video games.

1   Look at the verbs in blue in the *Memory quiz*. Put them in the correct column below and then complete the table.

Infinitive	Past simple form
see	saw

2   Do the *Memory quiz* with a partner. Who has got the best memory?

Memory quiz

1   What was the last film that you saw?

2   When was the last time that you ate in a restaurant?

3   When did you last go to a theme park or a zoo?

4   Where and when did you first ride a bike?

5   Who taught you at primary school?

6   How old were your parents on their last birthdays?

7   What was the last song that you heard?

8   When did you last make your bed?

9   What mark did you get in your last English exam?

10   At what age did you first have a mobile phone?

11   Who spoke to you first at school today?

12   What did you do on your last birthday?

13   Who gave you a present for your last birthday? What was it?

14   Who did you last buy a present for? What was it?

3   🔊 1.04   Study the key phrases. Then listen to four dialogues and answer the questions.

KEY PHRASES ○ Asking about the past

1   What was the last *exam* that you *took*?
2   When did you last *go to London*?
3   At what age did you first *ride a horse*?
4   What did you *do on Saturday*?

4   **ACTIVATE**   Test your partner's memory again. Write six new questions using the key phrases and your own ideas.

> At what age did you first see a film?

> I was four.

Past simple

1 Complete the sentences from the listening on page 6 with the words in the box. Then answer questions a, b and c.

> bought wasn't didn't were did started

I **¹__** scared, but I was nervous.
I **²__** some new clothes.
You **³__** young!
She **⁴__** when she was only six.
What **⁵__** you do on Saturday?
I **⁶__** see you at the sports centre.

a Which of the verbs are regular and irregular?
b How do we form the past simple of regular verbs?
c Which verb do we use to form negatives and questions?

(More practice ⇨ Workbook page 7)

2 🔘 1.05 Listen to Tina talking about a football match and answer the questions. Write complete sentences.

1 What did Jim give Tina?
2 When was the match?
3 How did they get to the match?
4 Did a lot of people watch the match?
5 Did Chelsea win the match?
6 How many goals did Drogba score?
7 Why was Jim sad?

3 Write true affirmative and negative sentences about you.

(go to a football match) last year
I went to a football match last year.
I didn't go to a football match last year.

1 (watch TV) last night
2 (listen to music) yesterday
3 (meet friends) on Sunday
4 (do homework) yesterday
5 (play video games) this morning
6 (ride a bicycle) last week
7 (buy a present) last weekend
8 (be at home) on Saturday evening

Object and subject questions

4 Look at structures a and b. Find three more examples of structure b in the *Memory quiz* on page 6. When do we **not** use *did* in a question?

a question word + *did* + subject + main verb
Who did you visit? I visited my aunt.
Which did you get, the bus or the train?
I got the bus.
(The question word refers to the object.)

b question word + main verb
Who visited you? My grandfather visited me.
Which cost more? The train cost more.
(The question word refers to the subject.)

(More practice ⇨ Workbook page 7)

5 Complete the past simple questions with object or subject question forms. Then ask and answer with a partner.

1 Who __ (sit) next to you on your first day at school?
2 What __ (you / talk) about?
3 Who __ (teach) you to read?
4 What books __ (you / read)?
5 What toys __ (you / have) when you were young?
6 What __ (happen) to those toys?
7 Who __ (cook) dinner last night at home?
8 What __ (they / cook)?

6 ACTIVATE Find out about things your partner did in the past. Use the ideas in exercise 3 and the question words in the box. Ask object and subject questions.

> when what who where why

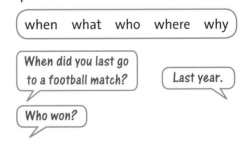

When did you last go to a football match?   Last year.
Who won?

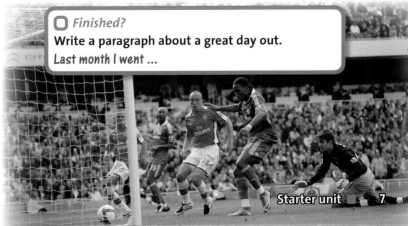

⬜ *Finished?*
Write a paragraph about a great day out.
Last month I went ...

1

Generations

Start thinking

1 What kind of hairstyles and clothes were popular in the twentieth century?
2 When were mobile phones invented?
3 When did a person first walk on the moon?

Aims

Communication: I can ...

- talk about my habits when I was younger.
- understand a text comparing generations.
- talk about events at different times in the past.
- understand people talking about memories.
- talk about past events and memories.
- talk about events in the past.
- write an account of a decade.

Vocabulary

- Past decades
- Uses of *get*

Language focus

- *used to*
- Past perfect and past simple
- Past simple and continuous

English Plus Options

Extra listening and speaking
Talking about a family likeness
⇨ Page 88

Curriculum extra
History: The Berlin Wall
⇨ Page 96

Culture
Britain in the 1960s
⇨ Page 104

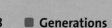
Vocabulary bank
Adjectives and prepositions;
Generations
⇨ Page 112

VOCABULARY AND LANGUAGE FOCUS
■ Past decades
I can talk about my habits when I was younger.

1 Check the meaning of the words in blue. Think of examples for each. Then compare with a partner.

TV is a great invention.

1 a great invention
2 a pop icon
3 a current crisis
4 a recent craze
5 a gadget
6 a place where there's poverty
7 a place where there's a war
8 a protest group
9 a booming world economy
10 a modern weapon

2 🔘 1.06 Do the *Generations quiz* with a partner. Then listen and check your answers.

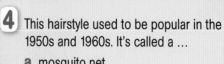
Generations quiz

1 The generation born between the 1940s and the 1960s were called 'baby boomers' because …
a the economy was booming.
b there were a lot of births.
c there was an energy crisis.

2 There were a lot of protests in the 1950s and 1960s. What did the symbol on this banner mean before it became the universal symbol of peace?
a End poverty.
b Stop the war.
c Ban nuclear weapons.

3 There are film, fashion and music icons in every generation. Both before and after her death in 1962, people adored Marilyn Monroe. She was a …
a film star and model.
b TV presenter.
c fashion designer.

4 This hairstyle used to be popular in the 1950s and 1960s. It's called a …
a mosquito net.
b beehive.
c spider's web.

used to

3 Complete the sentences from the *Generations quiz*. Then choose the correct words in the rules.

1 This hairstyle ___ be popular.
2 Most teenagers ___ have them.
3 When ___ people ___ to wear them?

RULES ○

a We use *used to* when we talk about a **past / present** habit or state which is the **same / different** now.

b The negative form is **didn't use to / wasn't used to.**

c We form questions with **was / did.**

(More practice ⇨ Workbook page 9)

---

5 These boots are called platform boots. When did people use to wear them?
a The 1960s.
b The 1970s.
c The 1990s.

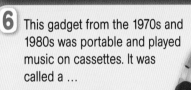

6 This gadget from the 1970s and 1980s was portable and played music on cassettes. It was called a …
a Runboy.
b Boom Box.
c Walkman.

7 Mobile phones were a new invention in the 1980s. But until the end of the 1990s, most teenagers didn't use to have them because they were …
a too expensive.
b illegal for under eighteens.
c dangerous.

8 In the late 1990s, there was a craze for Tamagotchi. These were …
a electronic pets.
b digital watches.
c video games.

---

4 Complete the sentences using the correct form of *used to* and the verbs in the box.

> send   listen   wear (x2)   play   have (x2)
> ~~exist~~   carry   be

In the 1950s ...
Video games **didn't use to exist.**

1 People ___ to the radio a lot.
2 TVs ___ black-and-white.
3 ___ people ___ emails? No, there weren't any computers!
4 People ___ phones in their pockets.
5 ___ families ___ games together? Yes, they did. Not many households ___ a TV.
6 Children ___ electronic toys.
7 ___ young people ___ more formal clothes? Yes, young people ___ jeans in the 1950s.

5 Complete the text using the correct verbs and the correct form of *used to.*

My parents were very anti-TV, so I **didn't use to watch** TV when I was young. In fact, they were 'anti' a lot of things. They often **¹___** to protests, but I **²___** with them. I stayed with my gran. She was a hairdresser and she **³___** my hair. I **⁴___** a really cool hairstyle in those days. It was great at her house. I **⁵___** bored. She **⁶___** the piano and sing for me.

6 **ACTIVATE** Find out about your partner's habits when he / she was seven years old. Ask questions using *used to* and the ideas in the box.

> sports   clothes   music   food   toys   gadgets

> Did you use to play football when you were seven years old?

> Yes, I did. What about you?

> No, I didn't. I used to play basketball.

○ *Finished?*

Think of changes in your life in the last ten years. Write sentences using affirmative and negative forms of *used to.*

I didn't use to send text messages when I was younger, but I do now.

1 🔊 1.07 **Which of these things do you think were common in the 1950s? Which are common now? Read, listen and compare your answers with the text.**

> ballrooms   big bands   mobile phones
> computers   jobs for women   discos
> black-and-white TV   bad language

2 **Read the text again. Write *true* or *false*. Correct the false sentences.**

1 The cinema wasn't popular in the fifties.
2 Alice's family bought a TV.
3 Alice thinks that teenagers are spoilt today.
4 Becky thinks that the fifties style of clothes was awful.
5 Alice doesn't like the violence on TV today.
6 Alice thinks that life is better for women today.
7 People get married earlier now than in the fifties.
8 Becky is respectful to older people.

3 **BUILD YOUR VOCABULARY Complete the sentences with prepositions. Then check your answers in the text.**

1 Most teenagers aren't keen ___ jazz.
2 She's sometimes shocked ___ the bad language and violence on TV.
3 She's cool ___ most things.
4 She's really interested ___ that.
5 I'm polite ___ older people.

4 **Complete the sentences with the prepositions in the box and your own ideas.**

> of   about   for   with   from   at

1 I'm not very fond ___ …
2 I never get bored ___ …
3 These days people are crazy ___ …
4 I'm not very good ___ …
5 Marilyn Monroe was famous ___ …
6 … today are very different ___ those in the fifties.

5 **YOUR OPINIONS Ask and answer the questions.**

1 How was life different for women in the fifties in your country?
2 Do parents spoil their children more now than in the past in your country?
3 Do you think people should respect the older generation? Why?
4 What do the older generation think about the younger generation in your country?
5 Do you think it's better to be a teenager now than in the fifties? Why?

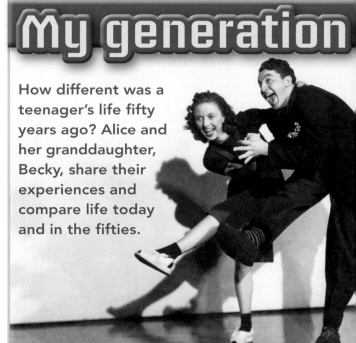

My generation

How different was a teenager's life fifty years ago? Alice and her granddaughter, Becky, share their experiences and compare life today and in the fifties.

Alice

'I was a teenager in the fifties. They were exciting times. A lot of terrible things had happened in the Second World War and when it ended in 1945 people needed to have some fun. Every Saturday, I used to go to a ballroom where a big band played live jazz. There was a craze called swing dancing, which we loved. We went to the cinema a lot, too. It used to cost two shillings then.*

Nowadays, there are so many machines and gadgets. I remember that a family in our street bought a black-and-white TV and we all went to their house to watch it. I'd only seen them in the shops before that. And of course, in those days we hadn't seen a computer or a mobile phone.

I find most young people today are respectful, but they want everything now. Maybe their parents buy them too many things.'

* Two shillings (1957) = ten pence

LANGUAGE FOCUS ● Past perfect and past simple
I can talk about events at different times in the past.

1

1 Study the timeline and the sentence. Write the events in the correct place on the timeline. Then choose the correct words in the rules.

I visited my gran last weekend and she'd found some of her old photos.

Earlier past | Recent past | Now

○ RULES

a We use the past perfect to talk about an action that happened **before / after** another action in the past.

b We use the **past simple / past perfect** for the more recent action.

c We form the past perfect with *have / had* and a past participle.

(More practice ⟹ Workbook page 9)

Becky

'I visited my gran last weekend and she'd found some of her old photos. They were interesting. I really liked the hairstyles and fashions, especially the big skirts and teenage guys in suits!

Things are different now. We go to discos, but we don't dance to live music there. Most teenagers aren't keen on jazz today and nobody watches black-and-white TV anymore. My gran is sometimes shocked by the bad language and violence on TV, but she's cool about most things. She thinks it's good that more women study and work now. She says women have more opportunities now. I want to do media studies and she's really interested in that. My gran left school when she was sixteen and got married when she was twenty. I think people wait longer these days. By the time she was twenty-two, she and my grandad had bought a house.

It's true that teenagers have got more these days, but I don't think we're all spoilt. Some teenagers can be rude, but I try to be nice and polite to older people because, like my gran says, I'll be old one day.'

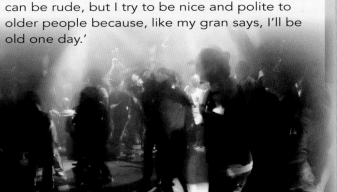

Pronunciation: Past tense *-ed* endings
⟹ Workbook page 90

2 Complete the sentences. Use the past perfect and the past simple in each sentence.

I **'d seen** (see) the film before, but I **watched** (watch) it again yesterday.

1 Alice ___ (tell) me that she ___ (not study) at university.

2 When her neighbours ___ (get) a TV, she ___ (go) round to watch it. She ___ (not seen) one before.

3 They ___ (not invent) computers when Alice ___ (be) young.

4 By the time he ___ (be) eighteen, he ___ (leave) school and ___ (find) a job.

5 The band ___ (not start) playing when we ___ (arrive).

6 In the 1950s, people ___ (want) to enjoy themselves because they ___ (have) a hard time during the war.

3 Complete the sentences using the past perfect and your own ideas.

The girl was in hospital because ... .

The girl was in hospital because she had broken her leg.

1 We were tired because ... .

2 By the time we arrived, ...

3 We went home after ... .

4 Before I came to this school, ...

5 When I got into town I realized ... .

6 My friend became crazy about ... after ... .

4 ACTIVATE Work in pairs. Find out what your partner had or hadn't done before arriving at school today.

I had eaten breakfast before I arrived at school today.

○ *Finished?*
Look again at the sentences in exercise 3. Think of different ways to complete each sentence.
The girl was in hospital because her mother had had a baby.

1 Complete the diagram with the words in the box.

> a driving licence better a bus up upset
> the flu on with

become
get married
get better
get ¹___

Phrasal verbs
get together
get ²___
get ³___ (like)

get

obtain / receive / buy
get a job
get a present for / from
get ⁴___

Others
get home (arrive)
get ⁵___ (an illness)
get ⁶___ (use transport)

2 Complete the questions with expressions in exercise 1. Then ask and answer with a partner.

1 Do you usually ___ early at the weekend?
2 Who do you ___ best in your family?
3 Did you ___ a ___ for your mum last Christmas?
4 What ___ do you want to ___ when you leave school?
5 Will your English ___ or worse this year?
6 Did you ___ on your first day at school or were you happy?
7 Do you usually walk to school or do you ___?

3 ⏺ 1.08 Listen to the dialogues. Match two words with each of the people in the photos 1–4.

> married upset uncle tickets party test
> uniform money

1 Michael – money, …

4 ⏺ 1.08 Listen again and choose the correct answers.

1 What did Michael do when he got his driving licence?
a He saved up to buy a car.
b He drove his friends to school.
c He went out and bought a car.
2 What was Maxine doing before she got to school on her first day?
a She was getting upset.
b She was having breakfast and crying.
c She was talking to her friends.
3 What was Clare doing when she first heard the music?
a She was going out with Dave.
b She was dancing at a party.
c She was talking about Bob Marley.
4 How did Joey and his uncle get the tickets?
a Joey's uncle got them.
b They were a present.
c They were a prize.
5 Why did Joey miss the goals?
a He wasn't paying attention.
b He wasn't a fan of Manchester United.
c He couldn't see the players very well.

5 ACTIVATE Find out what your partner remembers about the things in the box. Use the phrases in exercise 1.

> your first day at school
> holidays when you were young parties
> journeys primary school school trips

> What do you remember about your first day at school?

> I remember that I got up really early because I was so excited.

Looking back

1 Michael

2 Maxine

3 Clare

4 Joey

LANGUAGE FOCUS ■ Past simple and continuous
I can talk about past events and memories.

1

1 Match sentences 1–3 from the listening on page 12 with descriptions a–c. Which tenses do we use in each sentence?

1 I was watching the clock and I was getting more and more upset.
2 I was talking to my uncle when he scored.
3 He gave me the money and I bought the car.

a Two finished actions in the past.
b Two past actions happening at the same time.
c An action which was in progress when another action happened.

More practice ⇨ Workbook page 11

STUDY STRATEGY ○ Highlighting examples of tenses

2 Copy five sentences from exercise 4 on page 12. Then underline different verb tenses with different colours. This will help you to remember how the tenses are used and formed.

3 ● 1.09 Complete the questions in the *History quiz* with a past simple and a past continuous form. Then do the quiz with a partner. Listen and check your answers.

4 Complete the questions using the correct form of the verbs in the box.

> meet   do   eat   think   wear   ~~grow up~~
> use   ~~do~~   get

What sports **did you do** when **you were growing up**?
1 What ___ you ___ for lunch last Wednesday?
2 Where ___ you ___ your best friend?
3 When ___ you first ___ a mobile phone?
4 What ___ you ___ about while you ___ ready for bed last night?
5 What ___ you ___ at this time three days ago?
6 What ___ you ___ when you left the house last Saturday?

5 Study the key phrases. Which phrases can you use for things you have forgotten?

KEY PHRASES ○ Memories
I (can't) remember it clearly.
I remember ... -ing.
As far as I remember, ...
It was about ... years ago.
That's all I can remember.
I can't remember anything about ...

6 ACTIVATE Work in pairs. Find out about your partner's memories using the questions in exercise 4, the key phrases and your own ideas.

> I remember playing football when I was six.

HISTORY QUIZ

Where **was Usain Bolt competing** (Usain Bolt / compete) when **he won** (he / win) his first Olympic medal?

1 What new invention ___ (Alexander Bell / use) when ___ (he / say), 'Mr Watson, come here. I want to see you'?

2 When ___ (*Titanic* / hit) an iceberg in 1912, where ___ (it / travel) to?

3 When ___ (Neil Armstrong / say), 'That's one small step for man; one giant leap for mankind', where ___ (he / stand)?

4 Where ___ (Isaac Newton / sit) when he ___ (discover) gravity?

5 Where ___ (Mark Zuckerberg / study) when he ___ (invent) Facebook?

6 Where ___ (people / celebrate) the new millennium when they ___ (take) this picture?

○ *Finished?*
Write a paragraph describing your earliest memory. Use the key phrases in exercise 5 and the past simple and continuous.

SPEAKING ● Talking about past events
I can talk about events in the past.

1 Look at the photo. What do you think the relationship between Colin and Dean is? What are they looking at?

2 ● 1.10 Listen to the dialogue. Which part of the festival did Colin enjoy most?

Colin Did I ever tell you about the Isle of Wight Festival?
Dean No, when was that?
Colin Oh, it was around forty years ago now. I've got some photos.
Dean Oh, can I see? Were there many people there?
Colin Oh yes, there were over 600,000.
Dean That sounds amazing! Did you have a good time?
Colin Yes, we did. Fantastic! All the famous bands were there – The Doors, The Who, everyone. It was brilliant. But the best bit was at the end of the last day.
Dean What happened then?
Colin My favourite band was playing and a girl started dancing with me. Look – a friend took this photo.
Dean Is that you?
Colin Yes, and the girl is your gran. We got married two years later!

3 ● 1.11 Complete the key phrases from the dialogue. Then listen and check your answers. Practise the dialogue with a partner.

> **KEY PHRASES ○ Talking about a past event**
>
> Did I ¹___ tell you about … ?
> When ²___ that?
> It was around forty years ³___ now.
> Did you ⁴___ a good time?
> The best ⁵___ was …
> What ⁶___ then?

4 ● 1.12 Listen and choose the correct answers.

1 a It was the best bit.
  b It was brilliant!
  c It was around two years ago.
2 a I'm having a fantastic time!
  b What happened then?
  c It was a bit boring actually.
3 a No, when was that?
  b What happened next?
  c Yes, here it is.
4 a Yes, it was.
  b Last summer.
  c By 5 p.m.

5 Complete the mini-dialogue with the key phrases. Then change the words in blue and practise the new mini-dialogue.

Rose Did I ever ¹___ you about my birthday party?
Hannah No, ²___ was that?
Rose It was ³___ a year ago now.
Hannah ⁴___ you have a good time?
Rose Yes, we did. The ⁵___ bit was at the end of the party.
Hannah ⁶___ happened then?
Rose We hired a stretch limousine to drive everyone home.

6 **ACTIVATE** Prepare a new dialogue with a partner. Imagine that you were at a concert or a sports event. Practise your dialogue. Then change roles.

WRITING ■ Describing a decade
I can write an account of a decade.

1 Read the model text and answer the questions.

   1 What type of text is it?
     a A historical account.   **b** A narrative.
     c A news item.
   2 Which paragraph describes fashions in the sixties?
   3 Which paragraph describes what had changed by the end of the sixties?
   4 How many bad things does the writer mention?
   5 What event did millions of people watch on TV?

2 Study the key phrases. Which phrases introduce the paragraphs in the text?

> **KEY PHRASES ○ Describing a past decade**
>
> The ... was a decade which ...
> There were good / bad / difficult times.
> One of the most memorable ...
> In the world of music / films / fashion,
> It was the era of ...
> By the end of the decade,
> People were more aware of issues such as ...

Language point: Giving examples

3 Study the words in blue in the model text. Then complete sentences 1–4 with these words and your own ideas.

   1 There are some nice places near here ___ ...
   2 She watches reality shows ___ ...
   3 I like some unusual food, ___ ...
   4 Some English verbs are irregular, ___ ...

4 **ACTIVATE** Follow the steps in the writing guide.

The sixties was a decade which people remember for many reasons. There were good times and happy events such as music festivals like Woodstock. There were also difficult times, for instance, the Vietnam War.

One of the most memorable events of the sixties took place in 1969, when a person walked on the moon for the first time. Over five hundred million people were watching on 21st July when Neil Armstrong took the famous 'first step'. A tragic event which shocked the world was the assassination of President Kennedy in 1963.

In the world of music, there were a lot of pop artists in the charts, for example, The Beatles and The Rolling Stones. In cinemas, James Bond was a big hit. There were six Bond films between 1962 and 1969. Fashions were bright and interesting – it was the era of miniskirts, long hair and hippy clothes.

By the end of the decade, the world was a different place. People were more aware of issues such as women's rights and inventions like the calculator and the satellite had changed their lives.

> **○ WRITING GUIDE**
>
> **A TASK**
>
> Write an account of the 'Noughties' (2000–2009).
>
> **B THINK AND PLAN**
>
> **1** What positive events happened in the Noughties?
> **2** Were there any difficult or tragic events?
> **3** What music and films were popular?
> **4** What were the fashions like?
> **5** What issues did people become more aware of?
> **6** What new inventions changed the world?
>
> **C WRITE**
>
> Paragraph 1: Introduction
> *The Noughties was a decade ...*
> Paragraph 2: Events
> *One of the most memorable ...*
> Paragraph 3: Music, film and fashion
> *In the world of music, ...*
> Paragraph 4: How the world changed
> *By the end of the decade, ...*
>
> **D CHECK**
>
> • phrases for giving examples   • past tenses

Vocabulary

1 Choose the correct words.

1 During the energy **crisis / protest**, people had to save electricity.
2 Many people protested against nuclear **gadgets / weapons**.
3 Approximately 14% of the population of the UK live in **poverty / economy**.
4 Marilyn Monroe was a fashion **craze / icon**.
5 People suffer during times of **war / economy**.
6 My parents went to an anti-war **protest / invention**.

2 Match the sentence halves.

1 They're keen   a with football.
2 Tom gets bored   b by Dan's bad
3 I'm very fond   language.
4 Jill isn't interested   c at skiing.
5 I'm not very good   d on jazz.
6 Mum was shocked   e of chocolate.
                             f in science.

3 Complete the sentences with the words in the box.

> job   better   upset   married   up   present

1 It's Anna's birthday. I must get her a ___.
2 Dad got his first ___ when he was sixteen.
3 You need to take your medicine so you get ___.
4 She gets ___ when she sees programmes about poverty.
5 My sister got ___ in church last week.
6 I can't get ___ in the mornings.

Language focus

4 Choose the correct words.

1 When I got home I realized I **'d forgotten / forgot** my jacket.
2 By the time I **'d got / got** there, everyone had gone home.
3 We watched *Spider-Man II* last night. It's an old film, but I **saw / hadn't seen** it before.
4 We **hadn't eaten / didn't eat** dinner by the time Dad got home.
5 I didn't recognize Liz because she **'d cut / cut** her hair.
6 I didn't play in the match on Sunday because I **'d broken / broke** my leg.

5 Complete the sentences. Use the past simple or the past continuous form of the verbs in brackets.

1 Caroline ___ (go) into the shop and ___ (buy) a new mobile phone.
2 I ___ (get) really bored while I ___ (wait) for my friend to arrive.
3 My friend ___ (not give) me a present because he ___ (not have) much money.
4 Jack ___ (not watch) TV when you ___ (phone) him.
5 My favourite song ___ (play) on the radio and I ___ (start) to dance.
6 Lucy ___ (lose) her key while she ___ (walk) to school.

Communication

6 Match sentences 1–7 with responses a–g.

1 What music did you use to listen to?
2 Did you get upset on your first day at school?
3 Did I ever tell you about my first holiday?
4 The best bit was when we got to Paris.
5 When was that?
6 We had a party after our last exam.
7 Did you have a good time?

a What happened then?
b It was around fifty years ago.
c I don't think so. I can't remember anything about when I was younger.
d Yes, we really enjoyed it.
e Did you have a good time?
f We used to be crazy about jazz.
g No, when was that?

Listening

7 ● 1.13 **Listen to Jenny describing an early memory. Write *true* or *false*.**

1 Jenny used to live in the country.
2 Her earliest memory is from when she was four.
3 Her cat had caught a mouse in the house.
4 The mouse escaped and hid under a chair.
5 Jenny screamed and she and her mum jumped onto the sofa.
6 Her dad thought that the incident was funny.

1 Read the interview summary. Match paragraphs A–E with the interview questions 1–5.

1 What are your special memories?
2 What was different in the seventies?
3 What did teenagers wear then?
4 What music did you like?
5 What did you do in your free time?

Uncle Steve's life as a teenager in the 70s

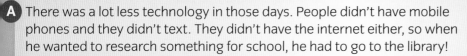

A There was a lot less technology in those days. People didn't have mobile phones and they didn't text. They didn't have the internet either, so when he wanted to research something for school, he had to go to the library!

B Steve was into bands like Led Zeppelin, Queen and Pink Floyd. He remembers that The Beatles were breaking up then. There weren't any CDs in those days. People played vinyl records on big record players.

C Steve and his friends used to ride bikes and spend time at each other's homes. There were no video games, so he used to read a lot of books!

D Fashion was fun and very colourful. Trousers with wide bottoms were trendy and skirts were all different lengths. It was fashionable for both girls and guys to have long hair.

E His special memories were of lazy evenings outdoors with his friends during the long hot summer of '76. It was so dry that there wasn't enough water and some houses had their supply cut off!

2 Write about an older person's teenage years. Follow the steps in the project checklist.

⬭ PROJECT CHECKLIST

1 Work in pairs. Think of an older person who you can interview (a relative, a neighbour, etc).

2 Prepare a short questionnaire. Include some of the questions above and your own ideas.

3 Interview the person and make notes of their answers.

4 Write a summary of the interview. Organize your writing into sections.

5 Find photos on the internet or in magazines to illustrate the person's memories.

3 Exchange your interview summary with the rest of the class. Did any other students find out similar information?

Happy together

Start thinking

1 What is an arranged marriage?
2 What is the best age to get married?
3 What is a first date?

Aims

Communication: I can ...

• talk about friends and relationships.
• understand a text about marriage.
• talk about how long I have done something.
• use extreme adjectives to describe experiences.
• talk about things that happened or started in the past.
• make and respond to invitations.
• write an email invitation to a friend.

Vocabulary

• Relationships
• Extreme adjectives

Language focus

• Present perfect + *just, still, already* and *yet*
• Present perfect + *for* and *since*
• Present perfect and past simple
• Present perfect simple and continuous

English Plus Options

Extra listening and speaking
Changing a plan
⇨ Page 89

Curriculum extra
Language and literature:
The realist novel
⇨ Page 97

Culture
Getting married in the UK
⇨ Page 105

Vocabulary bank
Verbs and prepositions;
Extreme adjectives
⇨ Page 113

VOCABULARY AND LANGUAGE FOCUS
◻ Relationships
I can talk about friends and relationships.

1 Read the situations in the text. Which do you think are the most and least serious problems? Write the infinitive form of the phrases in blue. Then check their meanings.

2 🔵 1.20 Listen to five people giving advice about the problems in the text. Match speakers 1–5 with the problems. What advice would you give?

The problem is ...

Mike: 'My family has just moved to a new town and I don't know anyone here. I've never felt so lonely. I've already joined a sports club, but I still haven't made any new friends. I don't know how to get to know people. What should I do?'

Estelle: 'I've just fallen out with my best friend. She's met a new group of people, but I don't get on with them. She goes out with the others all the time and I feel left out. Do you think I should make up with her? I don't know what to do.'

Sean: 'My brother got married last month. I really like his wife Angie, but now he's left home I don't see him very often and I really miss him. Has anyone ever had a similar experience?'

Paul: 'A friend introduced me to Tom a year ago. We became close friends because we've got a lot in common. But he's changed recently. He won't go out and he often sounds depressed. He's never been like this before. I haven't talked to him about it yet. Should I be worried?'

Kath: 'I've just had an argument with my friend. I feel sad because we've never argued before. She says that I'm too young to get engaged. She thinks I should concentrate on my studies and not get involved in a serious relationship.'

3 Complete the questions with the correct form of the phrases in blue in the text. Then ask and answer with a partner.

1 What is the best way to ___ new friends?
2 What have you got ___ with your best friend?
3 Have you ever had ___ with a close friend? How did you ___ up with him / her?
4 When you ___ with someone, do you forget about it quickly?
5 Should young people wait until they have finished studying before they get ___?
6 What is a good way to ___ people if you start a new school?

Present perfect + *just*, *still*, *already* and *yet*

4 Complete the sentences from the text and answer questions a and b. Then complete the table with sentences 1–4.

My family has **just** moved to a new town.
1 I've ___ joined a sports club.
2 I ___ haven't made any new friends.
3 I haven't talked to him about it ___.
4 I've ___ had an argument with my friend.

a Which of the adverbs do we use with negative sentences?
b Which of the adverbs always comes at the end of the phrase or sentence?

We know that these things have happened	We think or hope that these things will happen
My family has just moved to a new town.	

(More practice ⟹ Workbook page 17)

5 Rewrite the sentences with the correct adverb in brackets. Then add them to the table in exercise 4.

Has David phoned you? (still / yet)
Has David phoned you yet?
1 I've met the girl of my dreams. (just / yet)
2 You're lucky. I haven't met mine. (still / already)
3 We've arrived. (just / still)
4 Have you seen that new adventure film? (still / yet)
5 Pat has seen it. (already / yet)
6 I haven't been to the sports club. (just / yet)

6 ACTIVATE Write about things you have or haven't done this week using *just*, *still*, *already* and *yet*. Then find someone in the class who has done the same thing.

(I've already been to the gym twice this week.)

⬜ *Finished?*
Write four more problems for the problem page. Use *just*, *still*, *already* and *yet*. Then read your problems to your partner and exchange advice.
I've already failed two English exams this year.

Happy together ■ 19

1 When you read a text for the first time, try to understand the general sense of it. Look at the title and the photo. Then read the text quickly. Work in pairs. Tell your partner about the text using your own words. Summarize each paragraph in one or two sentences.

2 ⊙ 1.21 **Read and listen to the text. Write *true* or *false*. Correct the false sentences.**

1 In an arranged marriage, the parents of the future couple organize the wedding.
2 Imran hasn't told his parents about the girl he met on holiday.
3 Imran got on well with the girl his parents introduced him to.
4 Imran wants to marry the girl he met on holiday when the time is right.
5 Samina thinks that arranged marriages don't work as well as love marriages.
6 Samina thinks that a relationship needs more than love for it to last.
7 Samina says that perfect relationships only exist in films.

3 **BUILD YOUR VOCABULARY Complete each sentence with a preposition. Then check your answers in the text.**

1 He sometimes doesn't agree ___ me.
2 I'm thinking ___ going to the party.
3 She comes ___ Rome.
4 My cousin got married ___ a chef.
5 The match ended ___ victory for Liverpool.
6 My brother has fallen ___ love with my best friend.

4 **Choose the correct prepositions. Then complete the sentences with your own ideas.**

1 We sometimes argue **about / to** ___ …
2 It's difficult to concentrate **in / on** ___ …
3 It isn't necessary to pay **of / for** ___ …
4 I once dreamt **about / with** ___ …
5 I don't believe **of / in** ___ …
6 I try **to / for** ___ …

5 **YOUR OPINIONS Ask and answer the questions.**

1 What do you think of arranged marriages?
2 At what age would you like to get married? Why?
3 What wedding traditions are there in your country?
4 Are there any wedding traditions which you like or dislike?
5 What's the secret of a happy relationship?

Learning to love

How would you feel if your parents chose your partner?

In some cultures, parents choose a future husband or wife for their children and then organize a wedding. The reasons for these arranged marriages are complicated, but they're usually connected with status, traditions and money. This affects some young people in Britain, but they don't all agree with the practice.

I can talk about how long I have done something.

1 Complete the sentences from the text. Then complete the rules with *for* or *since*.

1 I've known her ___ August.
2 They've been with their partners ___ years.

○ RULES

We use ¹___ with the present perfect when we talk about the duration of a state or action.
We use ²___ with the present perfect when we talk about the point when a state or action begins.

(More practice ⇨ Workbook page 17)

'I want to wait until the time is right.'

'There's a girl I like. I've known her since August, when we met on holiday. I'm not thinking of telling my parents yet because it's nothing serious, but I'm not sure that they will understand if I bring a girlfriend home. I think that may be a problem in the future. My parents come from a country where families choose a partner for their sons and daughters. They introduced me to a girl "from a good family" recently. I hadn't met her before, so she came to our house with her mother and father. It was a very formal occasion because they all think that this girl will be my future wife, but we didn't have anything in common. I'm sixteen and I don't want to get married to anyone at the moment. I want to wait until the time is right and choose my future partner myself. It's difficult because I respect my parents and I don't want to upset them.'

Imran, aged 16

'All relationships require commitment.'

'I used to think that "love" marriages were better than arranged marriages, but I've changed my mind recently. I've met people who are happy in arranged marriages. Maybe they weren't in love when they got married, but with time they've learnt to love and respect their partners. On the other hand, some people who are in "love" marriages split up. They've been with their partners for years, but they fall out and their marriages end in failure. I think a relationship needs commitment. Love isn't enough on its own. The couple must be understanding and patient and build up their relationship over time. People can't just fall in love, get married and hope that everything will be perfect forever. That only happens in films.'

Samina, aged 17

2 Complete the table with the time expressions in the box. Then think of more examples and add them to the table.

last Thursday   I was ten   ages   2009
ten years   the start of the lesson
a few minutes   a week   January

since	last Thursday
for	

3 Complete the text with *for* or *since*. Add the time expressions to the table in exercise 2.

Cultural problems

I've known Imran ¹___ six months. We've been good friends ²___ last summer. We haven't had many arguments ³___ we met, but we argued last week. He's been strange with all his friends ⁴___ a while now. His parents have lived here ⁵___ a long time, but they think Imran should have a wife from their culture. He hasn't spoken to me ⁶___ we fell out. I don't know what I can do …

4 Complete the sentences with information about you. Use *for* and *since*.

(be) friends with …
I've been friends with Marco for six years.

1 (know) my teacher …
2 (be) in this class …
3 (have) a mobile phone
4 (live) here …
5 (understand) English …
6 (not have) an exam …

5 ACTIVATE Interview your partner about how long they have done things. Use *for* and *since*, the ideas in exercise 4 and your own ideas.

How long have you known your teacher?

I've known him since the beginning of the year.

○ Finished?

Write a short summary of your interview in exercise 5.

John has been friends with Marco for six years …

1 🔊 1.22 Match adjectives 1–9 with the extreme adjectives in the box. Then listen and check your answers.

> awful   outstanding   exhausting
> hilarious   gorgeous   unforgettable
> terrifying   revolting   furious   ~~fascinating~~

interesting **fascinating**	**5** frightening
1 tiring	**6** bad
2 funny	**7** memorable
3 angry	**8** good
4 good-looking	**9** unpleasant

(Pronunciation: Word stress ➡ Workbook page 90)

2 Work in pairs. Ask and answer 1–6 using extreme adjectives.

film / good? No

(Was the film good?)   (No, it was awful.)

1 journey / tiring? Yes
2 lesson / boring? No
3 dad / angry? Yes
4 food / tasty? No
5 TV programme / funny? Yes
6 exam results / bad? No

3 Read the ideas for great dates. Tell your partner which things you have and haven't done. Use adjectives in exercise 1.

(I've never done a bungee jump. It looks terrifying.)

4 🔊 1.23 Listen. Which three activities in exercise 3 do the people mention?

5 🔊 1.23 Listen again. Complete the table.

Person	Activity	When?	Who with?	His/her opinions of the date
Lauren	1___	yesterday	2___	terrifying, 3___
Matt	4___	5___	Kelly	boring, 6___
Lucinda	7___	8___	9___	10___, bad

6 ACTIVATE Find out about your partner's experiences. Ask about the things in the box or use your own ideas. Use extreme adjectives.

> film   day out   meal   party   night out
> holiday   book

(What's the most hilarious film you've ever seen?)

(Nacho Libre.)

Great dates

Some of our readers' ideas for great dates ...

do a bungee jump
go to a funfair
walk in the moonlight
play beach volleyball
go to the theatre

learn to dance salsa
climb a mountain
watch a horror film
go to a basketball match
eat sushi

LANGUAGE FOCUS ■ **Present perfect and past simple • Present perfect simple and continuous**
I can talk about things that happened or started in the past.

2

Present perfect and past simple

1 Study the sentences from the listening on page 22. Complete the table with the time expressions in blue. Do we use the present perfect with finished or unfinished time expressions?

1 I haven't been out much this week.
2 I've been out with Sam a few times this month.
3 That guy you met a couple of months ago.
4 We went to a play on Sunday.
5 Have you seen Charlie today?
6 I didn't see him yesterday either.

Unfinished period of time	this week
Finished period of time	

(More practice ⟹ Workbook page 19)

2 ● 1.24 Complete the text using the present perfect or the past simple form of the verbs in brackets. Listen and check. Then add the time expressions in blue to the table in exercise 1.

I **¹**___ (meet) Andy on a diving course when I was seventeen. We **²**___ (be) together since then and in the last six years we **³**___ (visit) some awesome places on our holidays. Last month, we **⁴**___ (decide) to get married. The wedding **⁵**___ (be) great, but exhausting because we were underwater and I **⁶**___ (have) a big wedding dress on. Since we got married, we **⁷**___ (not have) time to think or relax. These last few weeks **⁸**___ (go) very fast. Time flies when you're in love.

3 Work in pairs. Ask and answer questions about what you have done this year. Use the time expressions in exercise 1, the phrases in the box and your own ideas.

ride a horse   lose some money
swim in the sea   do any sport   eat foreign food

(Have you ridden a horse this year?)   (Yes, I rode one when I was on holiday.)

(When was that?)   (It was last July.)

Present perfect simple and continuous

4 Study sentences a–d and match them with descriptions 1–4. When do we use the present perfect simple and when do we use the continuous?

a I'm exhausted. I've been running.
b I've run three long distance races.
c I've been running for 30 minutes.
d I've always liked running.

1 An action that is finished and complete.
2 A verb which describes a state.
3 An action that started in the past and is still going on.
4 An action that has recently stopped and which explains the present situation.

(More practice ⟹ Workbook page 19)

5 Complete the sentences with the present perfect simple or continuous form of the verbs in brackets.

1 I ___ (read) one of his books, but I didn't like it.
2 I ___ (try) to phone Anna all day. Is she there?
3 We ___ (drive) for hours and we still haven't arrived.
4 Hurray! We ___ (finish) at last!
5 We ___ (already / see) this film twice. It's brilliant.
6 I ___ (look) for my keys for ages, but I can't find them!
7 How long ___ you ___ (learn) English?
8 They're terrified. They ___ (watch) a horror film.

6 ACTIVATE Work in pairs. Give explanations for 1–6. Use the present perfect continuous.

1 You look cold.
2 Her English is good.
3 You're wet.
4 The room's a mess.
5 The teacher's angry.
6 He's tired.

(You look cold.)   (I've been waiting for the bus.)

◻ *Finished?*
Think of some imaginative excuses for arriving late to class.
I'm sorry I'm late. I've been having dinner with Brad Pitt.

SPEAKING ● Invitations

I can make and respond to invitations.

1 Look at the photo. Where are Marie and Dean?

2 🔊 1.25 Listen to the dialogue. Does Marie accept Dean's invitation?

Marie Hi, Dean. I haven't seen you for a while. How are things?
Dean Not bad. How are you?
Marie I'm OK. What are you doing in town today?
Dean Oh, I've just returned some books to the library.
Marie Hey, I'm going to Tate's for coffee. Have you got time for one?
Dean I can't, I'm afraid, I've got to get home. Sorry!
Marie No problem. I haven't got much time anyway.
Dean Have you seen that new horror film yet? It's on at the cinema in town this week.
Marie No, I haven't, but I've heard it's terrifying.
Dean I'm going to see it with some friends tomorrow. Do you fancy coming?
Marie I'd love to. What time?
Dean I'm not sure. I'll text you, OK?
Marie That would be great. See you later then, Dean.
Dean OK. Bye, Marie.

3 🔊 1.26 Complete the key phrases from the dialogue. Which phrase is used to refuse an invitation politely? Listen and check. Then practise the dialogue with a partner.

> **KEY PHRASES ○ Making and responding to invitations**
>
> Have you got ¹___ for one?
> I can't, I'm ²___.
> Do you ³___ coming?
> I'd ⁴___ to.
> I'll ⁵___ you, OK?
> That ⁶___ be great.

4 Order sentences a–d to make a different ending for the dialogue. Then practise the dialogue again.

Dean I'm going to see it with some friends tomorrow. Do you fancy coming?
a Oh, I see. OK then. Bye, Marie.
b Oh well, maybe we can go out next week.
c I can't, I'm afraid. I'm going out with my sister.
d I don't know. I'm quite busy next week, too.

5 Work in pairs. Accept or refuse your partner's invitations to 1–5. Use phrases from exercises 3 and 4.

1 a sushi restaurant
2 a salsa class
3 a comedy film
4 the new shopping centre
5 a climbing wall

> Do you fancy coming to a sushi restaurant with me?

> I can't, I'm afraid, I've already got a date tonight.

6 **ACTIVATE** Prepare and practise a new dialogue with a partner. Use the information below or your own ideas. Decide if you want to accept or refuse the invitation. Then change roles.

The Twin Monkeys
at the Central Auditorium

Saturday 14 November
8.00 p.m.

VOTED NEW BAND OF THE YEAR!

WRITING ◼ An email to a friend
I can write an email invitation to a friend.

2

1 Read the model text and answer the questions.

1 Who is Carly writing to? Why is she writing?
2 Which paragraph gives Carly's news?
3 Where did Carly go last week?
4 Which paragraph gives details of the course?
5 How did Carly hear about the water sports centre?

To: Paul
From: Carly
Subject: Surfing course

Hi Paul

1 How are things? I hope you had a good time in Spain. Did you make any new friends?

2 I haven't done much since the start of the holidays. I've been relaxing at home most of the time. Things are quiet here because most of my friends have gone away. I've been out with Jan a few times. We went to a music festival in Kingston last weekend. It was good fun, but it rained on Sunday.

3 Have you made any plans for August? Do you fancy going on a four-day surfing course with me in the first week? Neither of us has been surfing before, so it would be a new experience. The course is at a water sports centre near Porthkerris in Cornwall and it doesn't cost a lot. Apparently there's a campsite at the centre and everyone is very friendly. My cousins told me about it. Both of them have been there and they say it's brilliant. I've attached a link to the course website so you can have a look.

4 What do you reckon? I think it sounds like fun. I really hope that you can come.

Let me know then.

Carly

2 Study the key phrases. Which phrase is used to make an invitation?

> **KEY PHRASES ○ Inviting a friend**
>
> Have you made any plans for … ?
> Let me know then.
> I really hope that you …
> What do you reckon?
> Do you fancy … ?

Language point: *both* and *neither*

3 Study the examples. Then write sentences with *both* or *neither*. Include the pronouns in brackets.

Both of them have been there. = plural verb
Neither of us has been diving. = singular verb

Paul is happy. You're happy. (you)
Both of you are happy.

1 He can't dive. I can't dive. (us)
2 Tom doesn't eat meat. Jo doesn't eat meat. (them)
3 Sandra is laughing. David is laughing. (them)
4 She isn't going. He isn't going. (them)
5 I've been on holiday. She's been on holiday. (us)

4 ACTIVATE Follow the steps in the writing guide.

> **○ WRITING GUIDE**
>
> **A TASK**
>
> Write an email to a friend. Give your news and invite him / her to a music festival or another event.
>
> **B THINK AND PLAN**
>
> 1 Where are you? What have you been doing lately?
> 2 What did you do last weekend? What happened?
> 3 What do you want to do with your friend?
> 4 When do you want to do it?
> 5 Where could you stay?
> 6 What is it like?
> 7 Who told you about it?
>
> **C WRITE**
>
> Paragraph 1: Introduction
> *… I hope you …*
> Paragraph 2: Your news
> *I've / haven't …*
> Paragraph 3: What you want to do
> *Do you fancy going … ?*
> Paragraph 4: Conclusion
> *What do you reckon?*
>
> **D CHECK**
>
> • *both* and *neither*
> • past simple
> • present perfect simple and continuous

Vocabulary

1 Complete the dialogue with the words in the box.

> gets   met   common   made   fell out
> introduce   know

Dan   Have you ¹___ many new friends?
Zoe   No, I haven't got to ²___ many people yet and I haven't got a lot in ³___ with the ones I have met. I really miss my old friends!
Dan   Have you ⁴___ Sally? She's nice. Everyone ⁵___ on with her. I can ⁶___ you to her if you like.
Zoe   Sally Fields? I've already met her. I ⁷___ with her on the first day!

2 Reorder the letters to make extreme adjectives. Then write definitions of the adjectives.

1 yigfiterrn ___
2 einrgltvo ___
3 scfaitinang ___
4 hrioiusla ___
5 rifusuo ___
6 eougrogs ___
7 rgfounetletab ___
8 tsoutanngdi ___

Language focus

3 Complete the sentences using the present perfect simple or past simple form of the verbs in brackets.

1 I ___ late to school twice this week. (be)
2 I ___ Sam since last February. (know)
3 We ___ a fantastic holiday in Spain last year. (have)
4 Sam ___ to the football match yesterday. (not go)
5 When ___ your parents ___ married? (get)
6 She ___ her lunch yet. (not eat)

4 Complete the sentences with the words in the box.

> yet (x2)   just (x2)   for   already   since
> still

1 David hasn't told his parents ___.
2 He's really happy. He's ___ heard that he's passed the exam.
3 I've been here now ___ an hour and Jim ___ hasn't come.
4 Have you met Ella ___?
5 They've been friends ___ they were little.
6 No, I'm not coming. I've ___ seen that film.
7 I've ___ been introduced to Vic. I didn't know her before.

5 Choose the correct words.

1 You look very hot. Have you **been running / run**?
2 How many times has he **been playing / played** this CD?
3 I'm excited because I've never **been visiting / visited** the USA before.
4 Have you **been waiting / waited** for a very long time?
5 We've **been seeing / seen** three films today.
6 I haven't **been listening / listened**. What did you say?

Communication

6 Complete the dialogue with the phrases in the box.

> I've heard   love to   time   for a while
> Do you fancy

Sue   Hi, Mark. I haven't seen you ¹___. Where have you been?
Mark   Nowhere. I've just been busy.
Sue   Have you got ²___ for a coffee now?
Mark   Sorry. I've got to get back. Maybe another time.
Sue   No problem. ³___ going to a concert tomorrow? I'm going with some friends and there's a spare ticket.
Mark   Who's playing?
Sue   It's a band called Spikes. ⁴___ they're really good.
Mark   I'd ⁵___. What time?
Sue   It starts at 8.30.
Mark   OK. I'll meet you there.

Listening

7   🔊 1.27   Listen to four people talking about their friends. Match speakers 1–4 with sentences a–e. There is one extra sentence that you do not need.

Speaker 1 ___   Speaker 3 ___
Speaker 2 ___   Speaker 4 ___

a My best friend didn't know anyone at school.
b I've never fallen out with my best friend.
c My best friend is very different from me.
d My best friend is getting married to my brother.
e I was angry with my best friend.

2

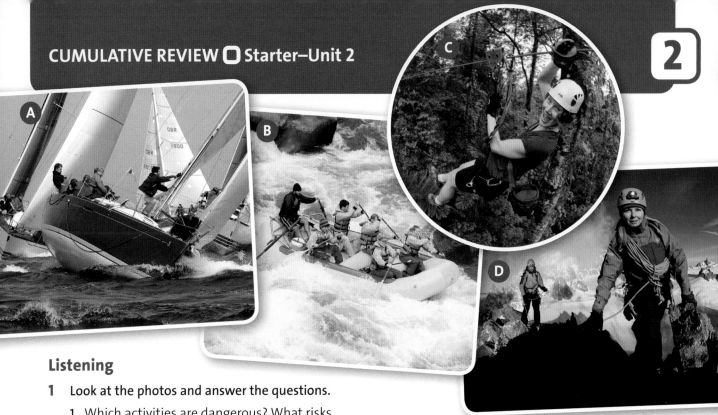

Listening

1 Look at the photos and answer the questions.

1 Which activities are dangerous? What risks are the people taking?
2 Why do people do these activities?
3 How do you think the people feel?
4 Which activity would you like to try?

2 (● 1.28) Listen to a conversation. What new sport has Max tried?

3 (● 1.28) Listen again and complete the sentences.

1 Annie was going too fast to see a lot of ___ when she was on the canopy zipwire.
2 Max went climbing with ___ other people.
3 Max met Dan when he went ___ last summer.
4 ___ has already climbed Mont Blanc.
5 They started the climb at ___ in the morning.
6 The view from the top of the mountain was ___.
7 Annie went sailing with her brother and his ___.
8 ___ had never been sailing before.

Speaking

4 Work in pairs and prepare a conversation. Imagine you are going on an 'extreme weekend'. One of you has been on a weekend like this before and is describing the experience. Answer the questions.

1 What extreme activity did you do last time?
2 When and where did you do it?
3 What was it like? How did you feel?
4 What did you enjoy most / least?
5 When are you planning to go on the trip?

5 Have a conversation. Use your ideas in exercise 4 and the chart below to help you. One of you is A and one of you is B. Change roles.

A *Did I ever tell you about … ?*

B *No, when was that?*

A Give details of the event.

B Ask what it was like.

A Describe your feelings.

B Comment on the experience.

A Invite B.
Do you fancy going … ?

B Accept.

A Suggest a date.

B Suggest another date.

A Agree.

Writing

6 Write an email to a friend. Describe your extreme weekend. Include details of the weekend and describe one exciting or frightening incident. Begin like this:

I've done something really amazing. I've been … with … .
We went … . It was the most exciting / terrifying / amazing thing I've ever done.

3

Health matters

Start thinking

1 When did doctors first use anaesthetic?
2 What do you think *zootherapy* is?
3 What are the secrets of long life?

Aims

Communication: I can ...

- talk about ability and possibility.
- understand a text about alternative medicine.
- talk about things that are possible or certain.
- talk about a healthy lifestyle.
- speculate about the past.
- exchange opinions with other people.
- write a discussion essay.

Vocabulary

- Medical science
- Phrasal verbs

Language focus

- *could, can, will be able to*
- *may, might, could, must, can't*
- Past modals
- *should, must, have to*

English Plus Options

Extra listening and speaking
Joining a health club
⇨ Page 90

Curriculum extra
Biology: Healthy eating
⇨ Page 98

Culture
Snack culture in the UK
⇨ Page 106

Vocabulary bank
Noun suffixes;
At the doctor's
⇨ Page 114

VOCABULARY AND LANGUAGE FOCUS
◼ Medical science
I can talk about ability and possibility.

1 Check the meaning of the verbs in blue in the *Health quiz*. Which words are similar in your language? Complete the table with the infinitives of these verbs and nouns 1–12.

1 operation	5 prevention	9 treatment
2 transplant	6 cause	10 development
3 suffering	7 discovery	11 experiment
4 cure	8 research	12 clone

Noun	Verb
operation	operate

2 🔘 1.33 Do the *Health quiz*. Decide which sentences are true and which are false. Then listen and check.

Flu epidemic 1918

Health quiz – true or false?

1 Before the 19th century, doctors could operate on people, but they didn't have anaesthetic. Many patients suffered terrible pain and died.

2 Surgeons can transplant human brains now.

3 Millions of people every year suffer from colds, but we still can't cure this common illness. In the future, we will probably be able to prevent people getting colds, but we probably won't be able to cure them.

4 Between 1918 and 1920, medical science couldn't prevent a flu epidemic which caused the deaths of approximately 50 million people.

5 In 1928, Marie Curie discovered antibiotics by accident while she was researching radiation.

6 Before the invention of X-rays, doctors couldn't treat people with broken legs or arms.

7 Scientists are now developing nanobots. These microscopic robots will be able to prevent and cure diseases from inside our bodies.

8 Scientists experimented with the first animal clones in the 19th century and in the early 20th century, they could clone humans.

3 Choose the correct words in the *Top ten medical advances*. Which do you think are the most and least important? Which are the most recent?

Top ten medical advances

1 A **suffering** / **cure** for malaria
2 The **cause** / **discovery** of antibiotics
3 **Developing** / **Suffering** a vaccine for flu
4 **Clones** / **Operations** to treat obesity
5 Drugs which **prevent** / **discover** depression
6 Heart **transplants** / **developments**
7 **Research** / **Cures** into the causes of cancer
8 Genetic therapy and **causes** / **experiments** with clones
9 The **development** / **prevention** of the common cold
10 A **treatment** / **transplant** for headaches

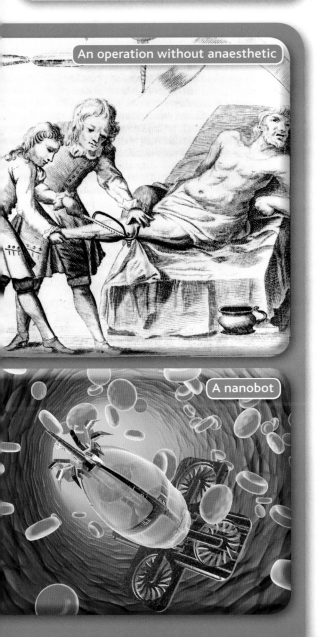

An operation without anaesthetic

A nanobot

could, can, will be able to

4 Complete sentences a–c from the *Health quiz*. Then answer questions 1–3.

a We still ___ cure this common illness.
b Doctors ___ operate on people, but they didn't have anaesthetic.
c Robots ___ prevent and cure diseases.

1 Which sentences express ability?
2 Which sentence expresses ability and possibility?
3 Which sentence refers to the ...
   a past? b present? c future?

More practice ⟹ Workbook page 25

5 Complete the text with affirmative and negative forms of *can*, *could* and *will be able to*.

Boy in a bubble

When Rob Thompson was born, he had a defective immune system, so his body *couldn't* fight against diseases. He ¹___ only survive inside a sterile plastic bubble or room. He ²___ play outside with friends. But thanks to a new treatment, Rob ³___ now do most of the things that he wants to do, although he ⁴___ live without special drugs.
In the future, scientists ⁵___ help other people like Rob with gene therapy. They ⁶___ improve the treatment for this illness and maybe even find a cure one day.

6 **ACTIVATE** Make sentences using the phrases in the chart and affirmative and negative forms of *can*, *could* and *will be able to*. Then interview your partner about their ideas.

| When I was younger, In the past, These days, Soon, I hope that one day, In the future, | I my best friend my parents people scientists | transplant brains use a computer explain the universe treat a lot of diseases live for 120 years speak English run 50 km/h |

I could speak English when I was younger. Could you?

No, I couldn't, but I could use a computer.

⭘ *Finished?*
Write sentences about past, present and future technological advances. Use *could(n't)*, *can('t)*, and *will / won't be able to*.
In the 19th century, people couldn't travel by plane.

1 Look at the photos and the title of the text and answer the questions. Then read the text and check your answers.

  1 What are the animals?

  2 How do you think they're helping to treat people in each picture?

2 🔊 1.34 Complete the text with sentences a–e. There is one extra sentence that you do not need. Listen and check your answers.

  a For example, they noticed that people who were ill usually became much happier when they were with their horses.

  b It can also be a very good cure for other behavioural problems like aggressiveness.

  c However, doctors who use these treatments are sure they help patients.

  d They agree that zootherapy can't cure everything.

  e Some skin diseases are difficult to treat with modern medicine.

3 BUILD YOUR VOCABULARY Complete the table with words from the text. What suffixes are used to form the nouns?

Verb / Adjective	Noun
specialize *v*	1____
treat *v*	2____
infect *v*	3____
ill *a*	4____
depress *v*	5____
lonely *a*	6____

4 Complete the sentences with a noun formed from the words in brackets. Use the suffixes in the box.

> -ion   -ness   -ist   -ence   -ment

  1 Is there a cure for ____? (sad)

  2 We can test people's ____. (intelligent)

  3 People get a lot of ____ from animals. (enjoy)

  4 There's a strong ____ between humans and animals. (connect)

  5 The doctor's ____ asked me to wait in the waiting room. (reception)

5 YOUR OPINIONS Ask and answer the questions.

  1 Which of the treatments in the text would you accept or refuse? Why?

  2 In your opinion, is it good for people to have pets? Why / Why not?

  3 Which do you think is better, alternative medicine or conventional medicine?

  4 What other alternative medicines do you know? What's your opinion about them?

  5 What alternative medicines are popular in your country?

Creature cures

Journalist Mark Elliott has been researching zootherapy: the use of animals in alternative medicine around the world.

It was in China that I first saw doctors using bees. A specialist was using the stings from bees to help people suffering from arthritis. The treatment is called apitherapy and although the stings must hurt, patients say that they feel much better afterwards because the treatment reduces the pain. In another part of the same clinic, a boy had his foot in a bath of small fish. The fish were cleaning an infection of the skin on his foot. ¹___ Research has shown that for people with these skin problems, this fish therapy could be more effective than creams and drugs.

LANGUAGE FOCUS ◾ *may, might, could, must, can't*
I can talk about things that are possible or certain.

1 Study the modal forms in blue in sentences 1–5. Then choose the correct options in the rules.

1 The stings must hurt.
2 This fish therapy could be more effective than creams and drugs.
3 Some people may find it difficult to believe.
4 They can't be imaginary.
5 It might be good for you.

◯ RULES

a We can use *may*, *might* and *could* to express **possibility / ability**.

b We use *must* and *can't* when we **are / aren't** certain about things.

c We **do / don't** use *to* after a modal verb.

(More practice ⇨ Workbook page 25)

In Europe, we've become more interested in alternative treatments like these in recent times, but Chinese practitioners have been using methods like apitherapy for thousands of years. The Ancient Greeks also understood the benefits of using animals to cure or improve certain medical problems. [2]___ They also believed that dogs could help cure certain illnesses.

This form of zootherapy is still popular. The patients of modern zootherapists spend time with domestic animals such as dogs and donkeys. It's particularly effective for people suffering from depression or loneliness. [3]___ The scientific reasons for this aren't 100% clear, but it seems that if we have contact with friendly, gentle, calm animals, we also become friendlier, gentler and calmer.

Some people may find it difficult to believe that these unusual treatments work. [4]___ The doctors say that the positive effects of animal treatments are so clear that they can't be imaginary, as some people suggest. So, if in the future, your doctor wants to treat you with a dog, some fish or some bees, don't be surprised – it might be good for you!

2 Choose the correct words.

1 You're improving. Perhaps you **might / can't** play in the school team one day.
2 Her leg **can't / might** be broken. She can still walk.
3 That experiment **must / may** work, but I'm not totally confident.
4 The treatment **could / must** be good. All the patients are better.
5 The weather is bad, but with luck it **can't / might** change.
6 Acupuncture **might / must** help you. I'm not sure, I've never tried it.

3 Make sentences using the modal verbs in exercise 1 and the words in brackets. Then compare your answers with a partner.

Sarah is crying. (in pain)
She may be in pain.

1 Your friend looks ill. (flu)
2 Richard is asleep. (tired)
3 They are speaking Spanish. (Mexican)
4 The teacher is laughing. (angry)
5 Lucy has gone to hospital. (ill)
6 Andy works in a hospital. (surgeon)

4 **ACTIVATE** Exchange opinions about topics 1–6 using the phrases in the box and the modal verbs in exercise 1.

be fun   be effective   relax you   be healthy
be good exercise   be boring   be difficult
be a good idea   hurt

1 acupuncture
2 doing a triathlon
3 smoking
4 being with pets
5 doing yoga
6 research into the causes of arthritis

I think that acupuncture might be effective.

It must hurt.

◯ *Finished?*
Choose five photos in your Student's Book and write sentences with the modal verbs in exercise 1. Then swap with a partner and guess which photos they have described.
I think the man might be eighty years old. He must be fit. (page 32)

1 Match the phrasal verbs in blue in *The eight-point health plan* with synonyms a–h.

a start
b visit
c reduce
d exercise
e recover from
f disconnect
g not have
h stop

The eight-point health plan

1 Give up smoking.

2 Cut down on sugar.

3 Go without a dessert sometimes.

4 Take up a hobby or sport.

5 Work out in a gym once a week.

6 Turn off your TV and computer more often.

7 Call on family and friends frequently.

8 Talk to people. It can help you to get over problems.

STUDY STRATEGY ○ Previewing the questions

2 Before you listen, read exercises 3 and 4 carefully and underline key words. This will help you to understand the dialogue more easily. It will also help you to focus on the answers while you are listening.

3 ● 1.35 Read the introduction to the *Live longer, live better* article. Then listen. What is a *centenarian*?

4 ● 1.35 Listen again and write *true* or *false*.

1 The Japanese lady hasn't stopped working.
2 James has to take up waterskiing.
3 Some of the people in the article smoke.
4 We should all give up chocolate.
5 Sharing your problems helps you to feel good.
6 All of the people have a similar attitude to life.

5 ACTIVATE Work in groups. Talk about how you could improve your lifestyles. Think about the topics in the box and use the phrasal verbs in exercise 1.

> sport and exercise   work   social life
> family   food   bad habits

> I don't do much exercise.

> Why don't you take up basketball or swimming?

Live longer, live better

How can you live longer? This week's special feature looks at super centenarians from around the world.

LANGUAGE FOCUS ● Past modals
I can speculate about the past.

3

1 Study the modal forms in blue in sentences 1–4. Then answer questions a and b.

1 She must have had a healthy lifestyle. She lived until she was a hundred.
2 He can't have done a lot of exercise. He's not very fit.
3 She could have given up eating so much junk food. She's lost a lot of weight.
4 My grandad might have smoked when he was young. More people smoked in those days.

a Which of the past modal verbs ...
... expresses a strong probability that something is true?
... expresses a strong probability that something is not true?
... expresses a possibility that something is true?
b When we speculate about the past, we make sentences with a modal verb + ___ + past participle of the main verb.

(More practice ⇨ Workbook page 27)

2 Rewrite these sentences in the past form.

She must live in the USA.
She must have lived in the USA.
1 They could be 70 years old.
2 He can't be a hundred years old. He's still working.
3 She might cut down on chocolate.
4 He must work out a lot.
5 She could go without dessert.
6 They might take up basketball.

3 Choose the correct words.

1 James couldn't finish the long-distance race. He **might / can't** have had an injury.
2 My grandma played tennis until she was 80. She **can't / must** have been very fit.
3 I'm not sure who phoned. I missed the call. I suppose it **must / could** have been my sister.
4 Sophia is early today. She **must / can't** have overslept.
5 Jacob looks upset. He **must / can't** have done badly in the test.
6 Elena is away on holiday at the moment. You **can't / could** have seen her yesterday.

4 Work in pairs. Take turns reading and responding to situations 1–6 using past modals and the words in brackets.

1 Sally wasn't at school yesterday. (be ill)
2 Bob looks pleased. (receive some good news)
3 Fred was heading for the tennis court and he was carrying a sports bag. (take up tennis)
4 Max has been in hospital for a long time. (have an operation)
5 Pete put sugar into his tea. (cut down on sugar)
6 Michelle has taken up sport and she looks much fitter. (give up smoking)

(Sally wasn't at school yesterday.)

(She might have been ill.)

5 🔊 1.36 Listen to five dialogues and speculate about what has happened. Use past modals to give your reasons.

6 ACTIVATE Work in groups. Look at the photos and speculate about the situation. Think about what has happened and why. Use past modals to give your reasons. Then tell the rest of the class.

○ *Finished?*
Imagine life in ancient times. Write sentences about people's lives, diets and health using past modals.
The Romans must have been sociable because they had baths together.

SPEAKING ■ Exchanging opinions

I can exchange opinions with other people.

1 Look at the photo. What are the posters campaigning against?

2 🔘 1.37 Listen to the dialogue. Which poster has got the clearest message?

Marie	Hi, Dean. Have you seen these?
Dean	No, what are they?
Marie	They're posters for an anti-drugs campaign. All the students in the school have to say which one's best, and why.
Dean	Oh, OK. Well, that one's only got text. To be really effective, it should definitely have a photo. What do you think?
Marie	I can't really decide, but I suppose the one with the photo has got a clearer message. Do you agree?
Dean	I'm not sure about that. I reckon it should be more positive. Of course the message must be clear, but it shouldn't try to scare us.
Marie	Mmm. You might be right.

3 🔘 1.38 Listen to the key phrases. Which phrase expresses a strong opinion? Practise the dialogue.

KEY PHRASES O Exchanging opinions

It should definitely …	Do you agree?
What do you think?	I'm not sure about that.
I can't really decide, …	I reckon it should be more …
I suppose …	You might be right.

Language point: *should, must, have to*

4 Look at sentences 1–5 and read the rules. Then change the words in blue using your own ideas.

1 You shouldn't smoke. It's dangerous.
2 You mustn't take drugs. It's illegal.
3 You don't have to diet. It isn't healthy.
4 You have to give your opinion.
5 The message should be clearer.

O RULES

a We can use *must / have to* to express obligation.
b We use *should / must* to express advice.
c We use *mustn't* to express prohibition.
d We use *don't have to* to express a lack of obligation.

(More practice ⇨ Workbook page 27)

(Pronunciation: Weak forms ⇨ Workbook page 90)

5 Work in pairs. Talk about opinions 1–4. Use the key phrases in exercise 3.

1 We have to use animals to test drugs.
2 We mustn't create clones of humans.
3 Drugs should be made legal.
4 Cigarettes must be made illegal.

6 **ACTIVATE** Look at the anti-smoking posters. Prepare a new dialogue about the posters with a partner. Use the adjectives in the box and the key phrases in exercise 3. Practise your dialogue. Then change roles.

(weak   clear   clever   direct   strong   subtle)

WHAT A
WASTE

WRITING ⬛ A discussion essay
I can write a discussion essay.

3

1 Read the model text and answer the questions.

1 Is the writer for or against animal testing?

2 Does the writer give both sides of the argument?

3 How many arguments are there for animal testing?

4 Which opinions in the text are the writer's own point of view?

2 Complete the key phrases. Then read the model text and check.

> **KEY PHRASES ⬤ Presenting arguments**
>
> There are arguments both ¹___ and ²___ ...
> One of the ³___ for ... is ...
> In addition, ...
> On the ⁴___ hand, ...
> All ⁵___ all, ...
> I am (not) in ⁶___ of ...

Are you for or against using animals for medical research? Explain your answer.

1 At the moment, it is legal in some countries to use animals for medical research. Many people think we should ban animal testing, *although* there are arguments both for and against this practice.

2 One of the arguments for using animals to test new drugs and medical techniques is that we cannot test them on humans. Animal experiments have helped to develop many drugs and medical procedures, like transplants. *In addition,* animal testing is efficient because animals mature faster than humans.

3 On the other hand, many people argue that animal testing is cruel. Also, they say that we should not test non-essential products like shampoos and cosmetics on animals because there is already enough information.

4 *All in all,* I am not in favour of animal testing, but it is necessary when there is no alternative. I believe that there should be stricter controls on research and experiments and scientists should develop computer models to replace animal testing.

Language point: Discourse markers

3 Which words or phrases in the box can you use to replace the phrases in blue in the text? Complete the table.

> furthermore   but   also   to sum up
> what's more   in conclusion   however
> on the other hand   even though

Adding	Contrasting	Summarizing
in addition	although	all in all

4 Choose the correct words in sentences 1–6.

1 This experiment is dangerous. **In addition / To sum up**, it's expensive.

2 **Although / Also** she was tired, she helped us.

3 You need to work out. **On the other hand / What's more**, you need to change your diet.

4 The operation is dangerous. **In conclusion / However**, there is no alternative.

5 You can have an operation. **On the other hand / All in all**, you could try acupuncture.

6 I've got your test results and **all in all / although** you have done quite well.

5 ACTIVATE Follow the steps in the writing guide.

> **⬤ WRITING GUIDE**
>
> ### A TASK
>
> Write a discussion essay with this title:
> Are you for or against vegetarianism? Explain your answer.
>
> ### B THINK AND PLAN
>
> 1 What's the situation at the moment?
> 2 What arguments for and against vegetarianism can you think of?
> 3 What's your personal opinion? Why?
>
> ### C WRITE
>
> **Paragraph 1: Introduction**
> *At the moment, it is ...*
> **Paragraph 2: Arguments for**
> *One of the arguments for ...*
> **Paragraph 3: Arguments against**
> *On the other hand, ...*
> **Paragraph 4: Conclusion**
> *All in all, ...*
>
> ### D CHECK
>
> • paragraphs   • discourse markers
> • *may, might, could, should*

Vocabulary

1 Write nouns for these verbs.

1 specialize ___
2 depress ___
3 suffer ___
4 experiment ___
5 develop ___
6 connect ___
7 prevent ___
8 treat ___

2 Complete the text with the words in the box.

> prevent   suffer   cure   research   development
> operation   discovery   transplant

Medical ¹___ has changed our lives. Before the ²___ of antibiotics in 1928, there was no ³___ for many common illnesses. Today, we don't ⁴___ when we have an ⁵___ because there are anaesthetics. These days, surgeons can ⁶___ many body parts and save lives. Vaccines are used to ⁷___ people getting some serious illnesses. The ⁸___ of new technology will help save even more lives in the future.

3 Complete the sentences with the words in the box.

> on   without   up (x2)   off   down

1 You should cut ___ on chocolate. You eat too much.
2 I can't go ___ salt.
3 My dad has got to give ___ smoking.
4 I've taken ___ yoga.
5 Please turn ___ the light when you leave.
6 She's going to call ___ her parents after work.

Language focus

4 Complete the sentences with the affirmative or negative form of *could*, *can* and *will be able to*.

1 I hope that one day doctors ___ cure all diseases.
2 When I was young, I ___ speak English, but I ___ now.
3 I ___ speak German because I've never had lessons.
4 I ___ go to school yesterday because I was ill.
5 My brother is very clever. He ___ read when he was four years old.
6 No, we ___ transplant human brains by 2020.

5 Choose the correct words.

1 Perhaps acupuncture **could / must** relieve the pain.
2 He fell asleep at his desk! He **might / must** have been exhausted.
3 Ann isn't here. She **must / can't** have forgotten.
4 You **don't have to / shouldn't** make a noise near the hospital.
5 She's walking to school. She **might / can't** have missed the bus.
6 He **can't / could** have gone home. He's left his bag on the chair.
7 We **mustn't / don't have to** learn Chinese at school.
8 Tania's in Spain. You **must / could** have seen someone else.

Communication

6 Complete the dialogue with the words in the box.

> suppose   have   sure   might   should
> think

Kate   Look at these adverts for the new science course, Nick.
Nick   Do we ¹___ to choose one for the school webpage?
Kate   Yes. What do you ²___ of this one?
Nick   It's quite well-designed, but I'm not ³___ about the message. It isn't very clear.
Kate   It ⁴___ definitely have more text. It shouldn't have so many photos.
Nick   What about the other one?
Kate   I can't really decide, but I ⁵___ it's quite effective.
Nick   Yes, I agree. But it isn't very interesting. The colours are dull.
Kate   You ⁶___ be right.

Listening

7 🔊 1.39   **Listen to a dialogue and write *true* or *false*.**

1 Emma and Dave are at a restaurant.
2 Emma is a vegetarian.
3 Dave is in favour of vegetarianism.
4 They both think that producing meat harms the environment.
5 Dave orders rabbit in cream sauce.
6 Emma chooses fish.

1 Read the leaflet. Match paragraphs A–D with questions 1–4.

1 What are the benefits of it?

3 How popular is it?

2 What is it and how do people use it?

4 How did it originate?

AROMATHERAPY

A People around the world have used products from plants and trees for over 6,000 years. Many ancient cultures, such as the Ancient Greeks, Romans and Egyptians, used them. The French chemist René-Maurice Gattefossé invented the name 'aromatherapy' in 1928 after he had treated a burn with lavender oil.

B Aromatherapy uses essential oils, which are concentrated liquids from plants and trees. People heat the essential oils and inhale the aroma, or they dilute the oil and massage it into their skin. You can also put a couple of drops of oil into your bath.

C Not everyone thinks that aromatherapy works. Therapists believe that aromatherapy can relax the body and brain, and that some essential oils are also antiseptic. On the other hand, some scientists say that there is no clear evidence of this.

D Aromatherapy is popular in many countries, especially in France. The essential oils are relatively inexpensive and easy to use. You don't have to visit a therapist to benefit from it.

2 Make an information leaflet about another type of treatment. Follow the steps in the project checklist.

○ PROJECT CHECKLIST

1 Choose a health or well-being treatment. Use one of the ideas below or your own ideas.

> acupuncture   herbalism   reflexology
> hydrotherapy   osteopathy
> homeopathy   shiatsu

2 Answer questions 1–4 in exercise 1 about the treatment. Find information on the internet or in a book.

3 Find some photos on the internet or in a magazine.

4 Write a short paragraph for each question.

5 Present the photos and text in your leaflet.

3 Exchange your leaflet with the rest of the class. Which treatment do you think is best?

4

Let's go!

Start thinking

1 What is your favourite kind of holiday?
2 What kind of space tourism exists today?
3 Where can you get tourist information about your area?

Aims

Communication: I can ...

- talk about holiday plans.
- understand a text about travel.
- talk about future plans and predictions.
- understand a travel announcement.
- talk about travel arrangements.
- ask for and give information.
- write about plans for a visit.

Vocabulary

- Travel: nouns and verbs

Language focus

- *be going to*
- *will* and *be going to*
- Present simple and continuous for future
- *will* for spontaneous decisions

English Plus Options

Extra listening and speaking
Buying a coach ticket
⇒ Page 91

Curriculum extra
Physics and chemistry: Satellites and spacecraft
⇒ Page 99

Culture
Volunteer holidays
⇒ Page 107

Vocabulary bank
Words which are often confused; Methods of transport
⇒ Page 115

VOCABULARY AND LANGUAGE FOCUS
■ Travel: nouns
I can talk about holiday plans.

1 Match the words in the boxes. How many compound nouns can you make? Then look at the *My Dream Holiday* quiz and compare the compound nouns with your list. How many more did you make?

luxury hotel, luxury accommodation

luxury guide return
sun diving mosquito
long-haul five-star
day city

equipment flight book
break ticket trip hotel
net accommodation
cream

2 Write definitions for six of the compound nouns in exercise 1. Work in pairs and test your partner.

You use this to find information about a place.   *Guidebook?*

3 Do the *My Dream Holiday* quiz. Do you agree with the results? Why / Why not?

STUDY STRATEGY ○ Extending your vocabulary

4 Add two nouns from the quiz to each list. Can you think of any other words which could go with these nouns? Compare your answers with a partner.

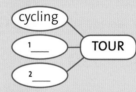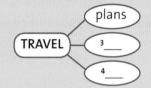

cycling ——— 1___ — **TOUR** — 2___

TRAVEL — plans / 3___ / 4___

My Dream Holiday

Do the quiz and find out what your dream holiday is.

❶ What is the first thing that you are going to do before you go on holiday?
  a Book everything with a travel agent.
  b Read lots of guidebooks and help my parents make all the bookings online.
  c Buy a return ticket and decide where to stay and what to do when I get there.

❷ You're going to visit Brazil. What are you going to put in your suitcase?
  a Suncream and a swimsuit.
  b Diving equipment.
  c A mosquito net and binoculars.

be going to

5 Complete the sentences from the quiz. Then choose two correct words to complete the rule.

1 I ___ stay in a five-star hotel.
2 I ___ camp or go on a cycling tour.
3 How ___ you ___ spend the time?
4 ___ you ___ take a bus trip?

> **○ RULE**
>
> We use *be going to* when we talk about ¹___ and ²___.
> **a** intentions **b** instant decisions **c** plans

(More practice ⇨ Workbook page 33)

3 It's 9 a.m. and you've just arrived at your destination after a long-haul flight. What are your plans? I'm going to ...
  a stay in a five-star hotel and sleep all day.
  b go on a guided tour of the city.
  c buy a guidebook and explore the city.

4 You've got seven hours between flights in Hong Kong. How are you going to spend the time?
  a Stay at the airport and read travel brochures about the city.
  b Go on a sightseeing tour of the city.
  c Visit the city on my own.

5 After a few days in the city, you plan to visit other places. Are you going to ...
  a take a bus trip to a seaside resort?
  b go on day trips to tourist attractions?
  c hitchhike around the country?

6 Choose the statement that is true for you. On my dream holiday I am not going to ...
  a camp or go on a cycling tour.
  b go on an ocean cruise or a coach tour.
  c stay in a luxury hotel or go on a helicopter trip.

Your dream holiday is ...

Mostly a answers: package holidays and city breaks
Mostly b answers: activity and sightseeing holidays
Mostly c answers: budget adventure holidays and round-the-world trips

6 🔊 2.07 Listen to Dave talking about his plans and answer the questions with full sentences.

Where is Dave going to have his holiday?
He's going to have his holiday in Greece.
1 How long is he going to spend there?
2 Who is he going to travel with?
3 Where are they going to stay?
4 Where is he going to swim?
5 What sport is he going to try?
6 How are they going to travel there?

7 Read Susie's email. Then write affirmative and negative sentences using *be going to*.

To: Dave
From: Susie

I got our plane tickets today. I can't wait! Paris in April is so nice and my brother Mark is great fun. He's into art and I don't mind going to some galleries with him. (No museums though!) He doesn't mind shopping – so we're OK.

Susie / travel / abroad in April
Susie is going to travel abroad in April.
1 Susie / have / a skiing holiday
2 she / fly / to Rome
3 her brother / travel / with her
4 they / visit / some galleries
5 they / go / to any museums
6 Susie / take / Mark to the shops

8 Work in pairs. Ask and answer questions to check your answers to exercise 7.

> Is Susie going to travel abroad in April?

> Yes, she is. She's going to visit Paris.

9 **ACTIVATE** Imagine you have booked a dream holiday. Ask questions and find out about your partner's plans.

> How How long Who What Where
> When How much

> How are you going to get there?

> I'm going to travel by plane.

> **○ *Finished?***
> **Write sentences about plans for a weekend trip in your area.**

1 ● 2.08 **Look at the title and the headings in the text. What advice would you give someone about these things? Read, listen and compare your answers with the text.**

2 Read the text again and choose the correct answers.

1 What should you remember when you pack?
   a A torch.
   b Your sports equipment.
   c Not to take too much.
2 What do local people appreciate?
   a Chatting with strangers.
   b Foreigners who speak their language.
   c People who tell them their life story.
3 How can you avoid getting sunburnt?
   a By keeping away from the beach.
   b By using suncream.
   c By getting a tan before you go.
4 What should you consider when you buy souvenirs?
   a Whether they are useful.
   b Whether they are typical of the country.
   c Whether they'll fit in your suitcase.
5 When's the best time to listen to music?
   a When you're travelling.
   b When you're alone.
   c When you're with strangers.
6 Why did the author write this text?
   a To warn about the dangers of travelling.
   b To give advice to travellers.
   c To suggest things to do on holiday.

3 BUILD YOUR VOCABULARY **Check the meaning of the words in the box. Then choose the correct words in 1–5.**

> trip   travel   journey   voyage

1 That was an interesting **travel / journey**.
2 The ship passed Neptune on its amazing **trip / voyage** through the solar system.
3 Space **travel / trip** will be cheaper in the future.
4 Did you enjoy your fishing **trip / journey**?
5 How did you **travel / journey** when you went to India?

4 Check the meaning of the words below and write an example sentence with each.

I forgot my wallet, so my friend lent me €10.
1 borrow / lend   3 spend / waste
2 look / see / watch   4 wear / carry

5 YOUR OPINIONS **Ask and answer the questions.**

1 Which is the most / least useful piece of advice in the text?
2 What do you think makes a good souvenir?
3 What items do you always pack when you go on holiday?
4 What are your favourite holiday destinations? Why?
5 What problems have you had on holiday?

What *not* to do on holiday

Luggage
You probably won't use half the things which you pack, so think carefully about what you'll need. You won't need a torch in a luxury hotel, but it might be useful if you're going to be camping in a field full of cows.

Sports gear
There's loads of stuff which you can hire when you're on holiday, like tennis rackets, a snorkel, skiing gear and so on. So you probably won't need to take all your sporting equipment.

Chat
Some people like chatting to strangers and others don't. So don't tell everyone your life story. Remember — the person next to you on your journey can't escape and didn't sit there to become your friend. On the other hand, if you're going to travel abroad, it's a good idea to learn a few phrases in the local language. People will appreciate it.

1 Complete the sentences and complete the rules with *will* and *be going to*. Then find more examples in the text.

1 I'm sure you ___ have a great holiday!
2 You ___ need skiing gear at the beach.
3 We ___ stay at the hotel for one week.
4 What ___ you ___ do on the first day?
5 Look! The train is leaving. You ___ to miss it.

Health

Think of your health as well as your image. It's nice to have a tan, but don't forget your suncream! You'll look silly with a face like a tomato! And you won't enjoy the beach if you get sunburnt on the first day.

Souvenirs

Memories of your trip are precious, but will you really wear that Hawaiian shirt in a month's time? And where are you going to keep that giant fluffy penguin when you get home? Maybe it's kinder to leave it with its friends in the souvenir shop. So avoid things you'll never wear or use again.

Customs

Different places have different customs. You won't be popular in a mosque or a monastery in shorts or a miniskirt. If you're going to visit a different country, find out about the customs before you go.

Music

Loud music will probably annoy your travel companions. It's great to have music with you, but for other people, your mp3 player sounds like you've got a gang of mad flies in your ears. So watch the volume or save your music for moments when you're on your own. And remember that a guitar is OK if you're with friends, but strangers might not agree that you're the next big pop star.

○ RULES

We use ¹___ when we talk about predictions about the future, especially after *I'm sure ...* and *I don't think*.
We use ²___ when we talk about plans and intentions.
We use ³___ when we make predictions based on something we can see now.

(More practice ⇨ Workbook page 33)

2 Complete the sentences using affirmative and negative forms of *will* and *be going to*. Which sentences are plans and which are predictions?

1 She's very sensible. I know ___ her train ticket. (she / forget)
2 We haven't got much money, so we've decided that ___ a holiday this year. (we / have)
3 ___ in a luxury hotel? (you / stay)
4 Be careful! ___ your drink. (you / spill)
5 It isn't a luxury hotel, so I don't think ___ a big swimming pool. (it / have)
6 The holiday was terrible. I've complained to the travel agent and ___ our money back. (we / get)
7 I think ___ hotels in space one day. (they / build)

3 Complete the questions using *will* or *be going to*. Then ask and answer with a partner.

1 people / have space holidays / in my lifetime?
2 your family / go camping / in the holidays?
3 our class / go on a day trip / soon?
4 you / visit the USA / next year?
5 you / travel around the world / in a few years' time?
6 you / buy a private jet / one day?
7 people / travel to other planets / soon?

> Will people have holidays in space in my lifetime?

> Yes, they will.

4 ACTIVATE Write down three things you plan to do after school today and three things you think you will do in the future. Then work in pairs and interview your partner. Find out about their plans and predictions.

○ *Finished?*

Write a summary of your interview in exercise 4.

1 Check the meaning of the words in the box. Then complete the sentences.

> book   board   check in   stop off   fasten
> turn back   set off   come across

1 Please sit down and ___ your seat belts.
2 We ___ on our journey at 9 a.m.
3 We'll ___ in Moscow on the way to China.
4 People with children can ___ the plane now.
5 The boat will ___ if the weather's really bad.
6 Tell me if you ___ anything interesting.
7 If you ___ flights early, they cost less.
8 How much luggage did you ___?

2 ● 2.09 Read the spaceship announcement below and choose the correct words. Then listen and check your answers.

> 'Welcome aboard from Captain 'Mitch' Mitchell and the crew. The flight **¹stops off / takes off** at 7 p.m. and the last passengers are now **²boarding / checking in** the ship. Our safety film starts in five minutes. Before this, can we please ask you to **³book / fasten** your seat belts? This flight is the *Tourist Special* and will **⁴stop off / set off** at the moon on the way to Jupiter, where we will arrive in about six months. We don't expect to **⁵land / come across** any meteor showers on this trip, but if we have to **⁶turn back / take off** or change course, we will inform you.'

3 ● 2.10 Listen to another announcement on board the *Tourist Special* to Jupiter. Who is making the announcement?

a A flight attendant.   b The captain.
c A tourist guide.

4 ● 2.10 Read the text and decide what type of information is missing. Then listen again and complete the text.

Cosmos 9 visits three places on its way to Jupiter. The voyage takes ¹___ months to reach Jupiter and arrives in ²___. On the moon, passengers can visit the ³___ and the ⁴___. The ship reaches Mars in ⁵___. The passengers spend ⁶___ days on Mars. Before it arrives at Jupiter, the ship stops off at Ganymede. The passengers stay ⁷___ nights there in a hotel. The trip from Ganymede to Jupiter takes ten ⁸___. The passengers won't meet any ⁹___ during the voyage.

5 ACTIVATE Work in pairs. Prepare a travel announcement for a sightseeing trip to the moon. Use the words in exercise 1 and the ideas in the box. Then present your announcement to the class.

> departure date   accommodation
> length of journey / trip
> activities and sights   stop offs

1 Study the sentences from the listening on page 42. Then complete the rules with *present simple* or *present continuous*.

1 The first night on Mars you're staying in the luxury Inter Stellar Hotel.
2 The tour starts at 2.30.

⚪ RULES

We can use the ¹___ to talk about schedules and timetables.
We can use the ²___ to talk about arrangements in the future.

More practice ⇨ Workbook page 35

2 ● 2.11 Study the key phrases. Look at the timetable. Imagine that you are in Birmingham station and complete the dialogue. Then listen and check. Practise the dialogue with a partner.

KEY PHRASES ⚪ Asking about times and timetables

When's the next ... to ... ?
What time does it get in?
Is that direct?
The next one leaves at ...
You have to change at ...

Birmingham	07.19*	10.36	16.20*
Wolverhampton	07.36	10.53	16.37
Stockport	08.09	11.31	17.09
Liverpool	09.09	12.09	18.15

* Change at Stockport

Passenger When's the next train to Liverpool?
Assistant The next one leaves at seven ¹___.
Passenger And what time does it ²___?
Assistant It gets in at ³___.
Passenger And is that ⁴___?
Assistant No, you have to ⁵___ at ⁶___.

3 Work in pairs. Prepare new dialogues for the situations below.

1 You live in Wolverhampton. It's 4 p.m. You want to go to a music festival in Liverpool which starts at 7 p.m. this evening.

2 You live in Birmingham. It's 9 a.m. You have a ticket for a football match in Liverpool which starts at 2 p.m.

Pronunciation: Third person singular
⇨ Workbook page 91

4 ● 2.12 Complete the dialogue with the present simple or continuous form of the verbs in brackets. Then listen and check.

Mum What time ¹___ (you / meet) John tomorrow?
Frank 8.00.
Mum 8.00? That's a bit late. The bus ²___ (leave) at 8.10.
Frank When ³___ (the next one / go)?
Mum Let's see. There's one which ⁴___ (set off) at 9.00 and ⁵___ (arrive) in London at 9.45.
Frank Oh, that's OK. There's no hurry. The match ⁶___ (not / start) until 3 p.m. tomorrow.
Mum ⁷___ (you / do) anything after the match?
Frank Yes, I ⁸___ (go) for a pizza with the team.

5 Complete the questions about a weekend trip using the present simple or continuous form of the verbs in the box.

stay visit get leave arrive take
eat see

1 What city ___ you ___?
2 How ___ you ___ there?
3 What time ___ you ___?
4 How long ___ the journey ___?
5 What time ___ you ___ at your destination?
6 ___ you ___ in a hotel?
7 What sights ___ you ___ on the first day?
8 Where ___ you ___ on the first evening?

6 ACTIVATE Plan a weekend trip to a city. Answer the questions in exercise 5 using your own ideas. Then interview your partner to find out about their plans.

What city are you visiting?   I'm visiting Paris.

⚪ Finished?
You are a tour guide in London. Write a paragraph explaining the day's itinerary for your tour group.

SPEAKING ● Asking for and giving information
I can ask for and give information.

1 Look at the photo. Where is Marie? What do you think she is asking?

2 🔘 2.13 Listen to the dialogue. How much does Marie have to pay the assistant?

Assistant	Good morning. Is there anything I can do for you?
Marie	I'm staying in Somerset and I was wondering if there's anything to see around here. Could you give me some information about places to visit?
Assistant	What sort of things do you like? There are some beautiful natural sites in Somerset.
Marie	That sounds good. Are there any day trips?
Assistant	Yes, there are day trips to the Cheddar Caves, if you're interested.
Marie	OK, great. Can you tell me if there are trips every day?
Assistant	I'll get you a leaflet ... Yes, here we are. They go every day except Monday at nine and eleven.
Marie	OK. And how much is the trip? I've got a student card.
Assistant	Let's see. Well, in that case it's £8. The full price is £12.
Marie	That's fine. I'll go on Thursday, then. Do I need to book it?
Assistant	I'll book it for you if you like. Can I take your name?

3 🔘 2.14 Complete the key phrases from the dialogue. Who says them? Listen and check. Then practise the dialogue with a partner.

> **KEY PHRASES ○ Asking for and giving information**
>
> Is there anything I can ¹___ for you?
> I was ²___ if ...
> Could ³___ give me ...?
> Can you ⁴___ me if ...?
> Yes, ⁵___ we are.
> Do I need to ⁶___ it?

Language point: *will* for spontaneous decisions

4 Read the rule. Find three examples in the dialogue.

> **RULE ○**
>
> We can use *will* when we make a spontaneous decision or when we offer to do something for somebody.

(More practice ⇨ Workbook page 35)

5 Write responses using *will* and the verbs in brackets for situations 1–5. Then practise the dialogues in pairs.

1 'My suitcase is very heavy.' (carry)
2 'I haven't got a timetable.' (give)
3 'I don't know how to put on my skis.' (show)
4 'Have you invited Ben?' (phone)
5 'Have you decided what you want to eat?' (have)

6 **ACTIVATE** Look again at the dialogue in exercise 2. Prepare a new dialogue with a partner. Use the information below. Practise the new dialogue. Then change roles.

Balloon Flights
See Kent from the air!
Morning flight 08.00
Afternoon flight 13.00
Every day except Tuesday

£80 adults
£50 students and senior citizens

Over 12s only please

WRITING ■ An email about a visit
I can write about plans for a visit.

1 Read the model text and answer the questions.

1 Why did Dean write this email?
  a To invite his friend to visit.
  b To ask for advice. c To talk about plans.
2 What are they definitely doing on Saturday?
3 What are the possibilities for the afternoon?
4 What is Dean's suggestion for Sunday?
5 What does he ask Jacinta to tell him?

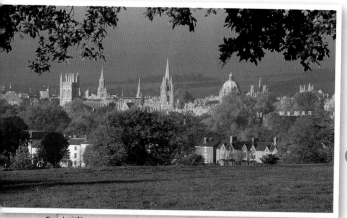

To:	Jacinta
From:	Dean
Subject:	Your visit

Hi Jacinta

1 I'm just writing to check that everything's OK for your visit.

2 I think you'll like Oxford. On Saturday morning we're doing a bus tour with my parents because they really want to show you the city. We'll be free in the afternoon, so we'll probably meet some of my friends, and we could either walk around the town or go to a museum. It's up to you. I expect we'll end up in one of the cafés in the shopping centre.

3 On Sunday, maybe we could catch a bus or train somewhere. There are some typical English villages around here, like Swinbrook and Burford. There isn't much to do there, but they're nice places. I'll get some photos and you can have a look.

4 We're going to meet you at the railway station tomorrow, so can you remind me what time your train gets in?

Looking forward to seeing you.

Dean

2 Complete the key phrases. Then look at the model text and check.

KEY PHRASES ◯ Presenting plans

I'm ¹___ writing to ...   I ⁴___ we'll end up ...
We'll ²___ free ...   Maybe we ⁵___ ...
It's ³___ to you.   Can you ⁶___ me ...

Language point: Linkers

3 Find the words in the box in the model text. Then complete sentences 1–5. Which words express a choice?

---

so either ... or but and because

---

1 We can have ___ a salad ___ a sandwich.
2 It's a pretty village, ___ it's a bit boring.
3 I'm writing ___ I need some information.
4 It's cold, ___ let's stay indoors.
5 Trains leave at 6.00 ___ 7.20.

4 **ACTIVATE** Follow the steps in the writing guide.

◯ WRITING GUIDE

A TASK

A friend from Britain is coming to stay with you for a weekend. Write an email about your plans for the visit.

B THINK AND PLAN

1 What are you doing on Saturday morning?
2 Do your parents want to do something with your friend? What?
3 What are the possibilities for Saturday afternoon?
4 Where can you go on Sunday? How can you get there?
5 What are the places like and what can you do there?
6 Where are you going to meet your friend?

C WRITE

Paragraph 1: Introduction
I'm just writing to ...
Paragraph 2: Plans for Saturday
I think you'll like ...
Paragraph 3: Ideas for Sunday
On Sunday, maybe we could ...
Paragraph 4: Reminder
We're going to ...

D CHECK

• starting and finishing your email
• linkers
• future forms

Vocabulary

1 Complete the compound nouns with the words in the box.

> ocean guide mosquito five-star
> travel long-haul climbing coach

1 ___ agent
2 ___ book
3 ___ flight
4 ___ net
5 ___ equipment
6 ___ hotel
7 ___ cruise
8 ___ tour

2 Choose the correct words.

1 Could you **lend / borrow** me some money?
2 The train **journey / travel** takes an hour.
3 Do you always **carry / wear** a watch?
4 NASA is planning a **travel / voyage** to Mars.
5 We **looked / saw** a snake in the road.
6 I only **wasted / spent** twenty euros on souvenirs, but I got some amazing things.

3 Complete the sentences with the verbs in the box.

> board check in stop off fasten
> turn back come across

1 You must ___ your luggage an hour before departure.
2 We ___ for three hours in Madrid.
3 Please ___ your seat belts.
4 The plane had to ___ because of storms.
5 Come on! It's time to ___ the plane.
6 Did you ___ anyone you knew?

Language focus

4 Complete the sentences with the correct form of *will* or *be going to*.

1 It's easy to find. You ___ a map. (not need)
2 Look at that black cloud. It ___. (rain)
3 We ___ our grandparents in the holidays. (see)
4 How long ___ in the USA? (she / stay)
5 I'm sure he ___ you to the airport. (drive)
6 I ___ very hard next term. (work)
7 Scientists predict that temperatures ___ all over the world in the next few years. (increase)

5 Complete the dialogue with the correct form of the present simple or continuous.

Joe   What ¹___ (you / do) this weekend? Have you got any plans?

Lucy   Yes. I ²___ (stay) with my cousin in London. She ³___ (take) me on a sightseeing tour of the city. I've never been before.

Joe   That sounds fun! ⁴___ (you / travel) up by train?

Lucy   No. I ⁵___ (take) the coach because it's cheaper. It ⁶___ (leave) at 8.10 and ⁷___ (arrive) at Victoria Station at 10.15. What about you?

Joe   Not much, but I ⁸___ (play) basketball at 2 p.m. on Saturday.

Communication

6 Match sentences 1–6 with responses a–f.

1 Is there anything I can do for you?
2 What time does the train leave?
3 What sort of things do you like?
4 I don't know how to get to the station.
5 I'll book it for you if you like.
6 How much is the trip?

a My sister will take you.
b OK, thanks.
c I'll get you a timetable.
d It's five euros if you've got student cards.
e I was wondering if I can book theatre tickets here.
f We enjoy visiting art galleries.

Listening

7 ⏺ 2.15 **Listen to a dialogue and choose the correct words.**

1 Tamzin is going to stay in **France / Spain** in July.
2 Billy's course begins on **15th / 13th** July.
3 Billy is staying **with a Spanish family / at a language school**.
4 Billy is going to spend **two / three** weeks in Spain.
5 Tamzin is going to camp **in the mountains / by the sea**.
6 Tamzin is having the party **in her house / in the garden** if it rains.

Listening

1 **Look at the photos and answer the questions.**

1 What types of holiday are the people in the photos having?
2 Which holiday would you most / least like to go on? Why?
3 Where did you last go on holiday?
4 What type of holiday is most / least popular with young people? Why?

2 🔘 2.16 **Listen to a conversation. Where has Annie been? Where is Jack planning to go in August?**

3 🔘 2.16 **Listen again and complete the sentences.**

1 Annie got back from her holiday on ___.
2 Tessa couldn't go on a ___ trip because she was ill.
3 Tessa got ill because of the ___ she ate.
4 They used ___ at night to prevent mosquitoes from biting them.
5 Jack is going to have ___ weeks' holiday in the summer.
6 He's going to go with ___ and his parents.
7 They are flying home from ___.
8 Jack doesn't usually like ___.

Speaking

4 **Work in pairs and prepare a conversation. Imagine you are planning a 'once-in-a-lifetime holiday' in a foreign country. Answer the questions.**

1 Where are you going to?
2 How are you getting there and how long are you planning to stay?
3 Where are you going to stay?
4 What preparations do you need to make and what will you take with you?
5 What are you planning to do there: sightseeing, day trips, cultural tours?

5 **Have a conversation. Use your ideas in exercise 4 and the chart below to help you. One of you is A and one of you is B. Change roles.**

A Tell B about your plans.

> B Ask for details.

A Give details of your plans.

> B Ask about preparations.
> *Have you booked … ?*
> *Are you going to … ?*

A Reply.

> B Give advice.

A *You might be right.*
I'll remember that.

Writing

6 **Write a tourist leaflet for a holiday destination. Mention things you can do and see there and how you can get around. Begin like this:**

… is a great holiday destination. There are plenty of things to see and do here.
A popular tourist attraction is the … .

5

Image and identity

Start thinking

1 Do you wear jewellery?
2 What is a *hoody*?
3 What is ethical fashion?

Aims

Communication: I can ...

- use reflexive pronouns.
- understand a text about attitudes to fashion.
- use the passive to talk about clothes and fashion.
- understand and react to an interview about ethical fashion.
- use the passive to talk about products.
- change something in a shop.
- write a letter of complaint.

Vocabulary

- Body decoration
- Commerce

Language focus

- Reflexive pronouns; *each other*
- Active or passive: introduction
- Passive: past, present and future
- Passive: questions

English Plus Options

Extra listening and speaking
Discussing music
⇨ Page 92

Curriculum extra
History: Child labour
⇨ Page 100

Culture
Punks
⇨ Page 108

Vocabulary bank
Negative prefixes; Fashion
⇨ Page 116

VOCABULARY AND LANGUAGE FOCUS
■ **Body decoration**
I can use reflexive pronouns.

1 Complete the table with the words in the box. Which of the things can you see in photos 1–7? Add more words that you know to the table.

> ~~piercing~~ necklace chain nail varnish moustache beard tattoo hair dye ring lipstick dreadlocks sideburns

Make-up	Jewellery	Hair and skin
	piercing – photos 1, 7	

> Pronunciation: Diphthongs ⇨ Workbook page 91

2 ● 2.22 Do the *Appearance and Identity* quiz. Then listen and check your answers.

Appearance and Identity

1 Thousands of years ago, ___ helped different tribes to identify each other.
   a hair dye
   b necklaces and other jewellery
   c lipstick

2 ___ were named after the American soldier and politician Ambrose Burnside.
   a Sideburns
   b Dreadlocks
   c Moustaches

3 In Ancient Greece, all men had ___. It was a disgrace to be without one.
   a chains
   b necklaces
   c beards

4 In some cultures, ___ indicates that an adolescent has become an adult. In other cultures, it's used simply for decoration.
   a a piercing
   b lipstick
   c nail varnish

5 In many cultures, couples give each other ___ when they get engaged. It represents eternity.
   a a ring
   b a necklace
   c a chain

6 Tattoos are an art form and a traditional symbol of maturity in Samoa. Young people ___ when they're twelve or thirteen.
   a tattoo themselves
   b tattoo each other
   c are tattooed by elders

3 Study the key phrases. Work in pairs. Talk about the body decoration words in exercise 1. Use the key phrases.

KEY PHRASES ◯ Appearance

... look(s) ... cool / painful / colourful.
I'd never have / wear ... .
I (quite / really) like ... .
I'm not mad about ... .
I don't like ... (much / at all).
I (don't) think ... would suit me.

> I'd never have a piercing because they hurt.

> Yes, I think they look painful.

Reflexive pronouns; *each other*

4 Complete the table with the reflexive pronouns.

> yourselves   yourself   herself   ~~myself~~
> themselves   itself

Singular			Plural		
I You	look at	myself. ¹___.	We You They	look at	ourselves. ⁴___. ⁵___.
He She It	looks at	himself. ²___. ³___.			

5 Look at the pictures and complete the sentences with *ourselves* and *each other*.

1 We looked at ___.   **2** We looked at ___.

(More practice ⇨ Workbook page 41)

6 Complete the sentences with reflexive pronouns or *each other*.

1 They'd both grown beards and they didn't recognize ___.
2 Emily has bought ___ some nail varnish.
3 I talk to ___ a lot. People think I'm crazy.
4 My flatmates don't like ___. They never talk.
5 He's taught ___ how to play the guitar.
6 My brothers cut their hair ___. That's why they look terrible!

7 **ACTIVATE** Complete the sentences with your own ideas. Include a reflexive pronoun or *each other* in each sentence. Then compare your answers with a partner.

1 My best friend and I have known ___ ... .
2 I hurt ___ once when ... .
3 My friend has taught ___ to ... .
4 ... and ... get on really well with ___.
5 We really enjoyed ___ when we ... .
6 We should look after ___ because ... .

◯ Finished?
Write a paragraph describing the appearance of three people you know. Use words in exercise 1.

READING ● Fashion

I can understand a text about attitudes to fashion.

1 Read the words in the box. Which of the clothes can you see in the pictures?

> baggy jeans   a miniskirt   a top hat
> a hooded sweatshirt   underwear
> a suit and tie

2 🔊 2.23   Read the title of the text and look at the pictures. What do you think the text will be about? Choose a, b or c. Then read, listen and check your answer.

    a Fashionable criminals.
    b Clothes that shock people.
    c Famous fashion designers.

3 Read the text again and write *true* or *false*. Correct the false statements.

    1 It's always people, not their clothes, which provoke negative reactions.
    2 People were scared by the top hat.
    3 Trousers weren't usually worn by women until the 1960s.
    4 All skirts and trousers were accepted in the 1960s.
    5 The author thinks that it's bad to wear hoodies.
    6 Some people have a negative opinion of hip hop fans.
    7 The author thinks that we should look at people's clothes before we judge their character.

4 **BUILD YOUR VOCABULARY** Find the negative form of adjectives 1–6 in the text. Then complete the table.

    1 moral   **3** responsible   **5** decent
    2 fair   **4** legal   **6** respectful

Prefix	Adjective	Negative adjective
im-	moral	immoral

5 Check the meaning of the adjectives in the box. Add negative prefixes and include them in the table in exercise 4. Then think of an example sentence for each word.

> common   regular   possible   sensitive
> organized   legible

6 **YOUR OPINIONS** Ask and answer the questions.

    1 What do you think about hoodies and baggy jeans?
    2 Are any fashions shocking these days? Why?
    3 What do you think of the way people dress in your country?
    4 What kind of clothes do you like wearing?
    5 What do your parents think about your clothes?

Clothes Crimes

Clothes can be comfortable and casual, smart and stylish, or colourful and eccentric. That's fine, but beware if what you're wearing is too different or daring. It isn't your personality or opinions, but your appearance that can cause disapproval. Clothes, it seems, can sometimes provoke a strong reaction.

There are many examples of clothes which have attracted the attention of the law. The inventor of the top hat, for example, was arrested in London in 1797 for wearing 'a tall structure calculated to frighten timid people'. People screamed and panicked when they saw it. Women have also caused controversy with their clothes. In 1926, the actress Marlene Dietrich wore a man's suit and tie in Paris and was warned that her clothes were causing offence. It wasn't until the sixties that trousers were accepted as part of a woman's wardrobe, even though women of all ages wear trousers these days. Miniskirts caused similar shock waves in the sixties because some people thought they were 'immoral'.

1 Compare the active and passive sentences in the tables. Then write *true* or *false* for 1–3. Find more examples of passive sentences in the text.

Active			
Subject	Verb	Object	Other words
Police	arrested	him	in London.
Women	wear	trousers	these days.

Passive				
Subject	*be*	Past participle	*by* + agent	Other words
He	was	arrested	(by police)	in London.
Trousers	are	worn	by women	these days.

1 We often use the passive when the action is more important than the person who does it.
2 The subject in active sentences becomes the agent in the passive.
3 The agent is always needed in passive sentences.

(More practice ⟹ Workbook page 41)

You may think that people are more open-minded now. But that isn't always true. Recent clothes 'criminals' were teenagers wearing fairly standard clothes. In Britain, young people wearing hooded sweatshirts were banned from some shopping centres because 'hoodies' are sometimes worn by criminals who want to hide their faces. But does that mean that all people who wear hoodies are criminals? It seems unfair and irresponsible to persecute people if they simply want to wear practical, comfortable clothes.

And in the United States, it was baggy jeans that shocked the public. A popular fashion with hip hop fans is to wear very baggy jeans and show their underwear – an 'outrage' which was banned and became illegal in some American towns. This probably wasn't because the clothes were indecent or immoral, but because some people thought that this style was typical of the disrespectful or criminal nature of some hip hop fans. Maybe the day will come when people will be judged on who they are and not on the clothes that they wear.

2 Complete the sentences using the correct active or passive form of the verbs in brackets.

1 These days, people ___ a lot of clothes on the internet. (buy)
2 The first wellington boots ___ by the Duke of Wellington in the early 19th century. (wear)
3 In the eighteenth century, new machinery ___ which revolutionized the textile industry. (invent)
4 A lot of cheap clothing ___ in Thailand these days. (make)
5 Very thin models ___ in some fashion shows. (ban)
6 Torn jeans ___ a popular fashion in the 1970s. (become)

3 Make the active sentences passive. Include the agent if necessary.

Did you know?

1 Someone named the bikini after an island in the Pacific Ocean.
2 Sarah Burton designed Kate Middleton's wedding dress.
3 Charles Worth established the first fashion house in Paris in 1858.
4 Nike sponsors the top US tennis player, Serena Williams.
5 People made the first jeans in Genoa, Italy.
6 Scottish men often wear a traditional skirt, or kilt.

4 ACTIVATE Write three true passive sentences and three false passive sentences about the *Clothes Crimes* text. Then read your sentences to a partner. Guess if your partner's sentences are true or false.

Miniskirts were invented in 1797.

False!

🔲 *Finished?*
Write example sentences for the vocabulary in exercise 1. Use the passive.
Baggy jeans are worn by teenagers.

1 Complete the table with nouns and the infinitive form of the verbs. Read the *Unethical fashion* article and check your answers. How are the nouns formed?

Noun	Verb
grower	grow
1 ___	produce
2 ___	work
manufacturer	3 ___
importer	4 ___
exporter	5 ___
6 ___	shop
7 ___	design
8 ___	supply

STUDY STRATEGY ◯ Prediction

2 ⏺ 2.24 You are going to hear an interview with Stella Franks. Read the *Unethical fashion* article again and try to predict the answers to the questions (1–3). Then listen to the interview and check your answers.

1 Why was Stella invited to the interview?
2 How much are workers in the clothes industry paid?
3 Will more clothes be recycled in the future?

3 ⏺ 2.24 Listen to the interview again and choose the correct answers.

1 The purpose of Stella's article is to ___ people.
   a shock   b inform   c change
2 The chemicals which are used to produce clothes are …
   a dangerous.   b recycled.   c expensive.
3 Shoppers can reduce the use of chemicals by buying ___ clothes.
   a designer   b Fair Trade   c organic
4 Fair Trade clothes are more expensive because …
   a they are made by famous designers.
   b the workers are paid higher wages.
   c they are made of organic cotton.
5 People shouldn't ___ old clothes.
   a throw away   b recycle   c buy
6 Stella is ___ about the future of ethical fashion.
   a negative   b uncertain   c positive

4 ACTIVATE Work in groups. Think about the problems described in this lesson. Discuss how the people in exercise 1 could help to solve these problems.

> I think shoppers should …

> It would be better if the growers …

Unethical fashion

The Jeans Journey: cotton, chemicals and costs
by Stella Franks, eco-designer

- Cotton is grown in many countries around the world. In some African countries, it is the main agricultural crop.
- 25% of all the world's pesticides are used by cotton growers.
- These days, producers use special chemicals to make denim soft. These chemicals can harm the environment and they are dangerous for workers.
- Clothes such as jeans are often manufactured in foreign countries. When clothes are imported and exported, they are often sent thousands of miles by ship or plane, using a lot of oil and petrol.
- Shoppers want cheaper clothes as well as clothes made by top designers. When prices in shops are low, suppliers and workers are paid less.
- When clothes are cheap, we buy more than we need. More clothes are thrown away and they aren't recycled very often.

Passive: past, present and future

1 Study the sentences from the listening on page 52. Which of these sentences refers to the past, present and future? Which part of the sentence changes?

1 A lot of chemicals are used when jeans are produced.
2 The article was written to shock people.
3 In the future, old clothes won't be thrown away.

2 Complete the sentences with the correct passive form of the verb in brackets.

1 190 million items of clothing ___ each year. (throw away)
2 More clothes ___ from the Far East in the next five years. (import)
3 Most of the cotton which ___ in the fashion industry ___ organically. (use, not grow)
4 The first platform boots ___ in the sixteenth century and ___ 'chopines'. (wear, call)
5 Roman clothing ___ in different sizes, it ___ together. (not make, tie)
6 In a few years' time, new fabric ___ which can generate power for your mp3 player using thermal energy. (develop)

3 ● 2.25 Complete the text. Use past, present and future passive forms. Then listen and check.

Famous clothes

Special clothes **are** often **made** (make) for films. These clothes ¹___ (create) by costume designers, who find out what clothes ²___ (wear) in different periods of history.

After the clothes ³___ (wear) by the actors, they ⁴___ (usually / keep) by the studios. Occasionally, however, they ⁵___ (sell) at auctions. This jacket, for example, ⁶___ (wear) by actor Johnny Depp in *Pirates of the Caribbean*. It ⁷___ (sell) for £12,367.

If you want to wear your favourite star's clothes, then search the internet, as more clothes ⁸___ (auction) in charity sales. These sales ⁹___ (often / advertise) online.

Passive: questions

4 Study the sentences from page 52 and answer questions 1 and 2.

a How much are workers in the clothes industry paid?
b Why was Stella invited to the interview?
c Will more clothes be recycled in the future?

1 Which of these questions refers to the ...
   a past?   b present?   c future?
2 Where do we put *be* in questions in the future form?

(More practice ⇨ Workbook page 43)

5 Order the words to make passive questions. Then ask and answer with a partner.

1 manufactured / in your region / are / what products / ?
2 when / built / was / your house / ?
3 students / will / taught / be / in the future / by robots / ?
4 was / who / this book / by / written / ?
5 when / miniskirts / worn / first / were / ?
6 what / be / new gadgets / invented / 2030 / will / in / ?

6 ACTIVATE Work in pairs. Imagine that you own a company that makes one of the products in the box. Complete questions 1–7 using the passive and prepare answers about your company and your product. Then find another pair and interview them to find out about their company.

(clothes   electronic gadgets   cars)

1 What ___ your product ___ ? (call)
2 Who ___ (*your product*) ___ by? (design)
3 Where ___ it ___ ? (sell)
4 Where ___ it ___? (advertise)
5 Which famous people ___ (*your product*) ___ by? (wear / use / drive)
6 Where ___ it ___ ? (produce)
7 Where ___ (*your product*) ___ to in the future? (export)

☐ *Finished?*
Design a leaflet to advertise your company in exercise 6. Write a paragraph describing your product. Include passive sentences.

SPEAKING ▪ Changing something in a shop
I can change something in a shop.

1 Look at the photo. What is Marie doing?

2 🔘 2.26 Listen to the dialogue. What does Marie want to change? What does she get instead?

Assistant	Hello. Are you OK there?
Marie	Yes, hi. I was given these jeans as a present, but they don't fit. They're too small. Is it OK if I change them?
Assistant	That should be OK. Have you got the receipt?
Marie	Yes, here you are.
Assistant	OK. Well actually, we've sold out of those jeans, I'm afraid. You can choose something else if you like.
Marie	Oh, right. … Can I try these things on?
Assistant	Yes, sure. The changing rooms are over there.
	…
Marie	What do you think of this coat? It isn't too long, is it?
Assistant	No, I don't think so. It really suits you.
Marie	I'm not sure about the colour.
Assistant	We've got it in dark red as well.
Marie	Oh, I like the red one. I'll take it then, thanks.

3 Study the key phrases. Who says the phrases? Practise the dialogue.

> **KEY PHRASES ○ Changing clothes**
>
> They don't fit.
> Is it OK if I change them?
> Have you got the receipt?
> We've sold out of those, I'm afraid.
> Can I try these things on?
> It really suits you.
> I'll take it then.

4 🔘 2.27 Listen and choose the correct answers.

1. a No, they really suit you.
    b No, I like the blue ones.
    c They aren't baggy.
2. a It doesn't fit.
    b Have you got the receipt?
    c Yes, here you are.
3. a Oh, OK. Can I try these on instead?
    b I really like the style.
    c The changing rooms are over there.
4. a No, I don't think so.
    b We've got them in blue as well.
    c Yes, sure.
5. a I'll take it then.
    b Yes, it suits you.
    c You can choose something else.

5 🔘 2.28 Look again at the key phrases and complete the mini-dialogues. Then listen and check. Practise the mini-dialogues for situations 1–4 with a partner.

1. **Tim**   Is it OK if I ¹___ this T-shirt? I don't like the colour.
   Assistant That should be OK. Have you got ²___?
   Tim   Yes, here you are.

2. **Jan**   This top ³___ fit. Is it OK if I ⁴___?
   Assistant We've ⁵___ of those, I'm afraid. You can choose another one if you like.
   Jan   Right. Can I ⁶___ this one on?
   Assistant Sure. The ⁷___ are over there.

1 jacket / too small   3 sunglasses / too big
2 trousers / don't fit   4 watch / wrong colour

6 **ACTIVATE** Read the situation below. Prepare a dialogue with a partner. Practise your dialogue. Then change roles.

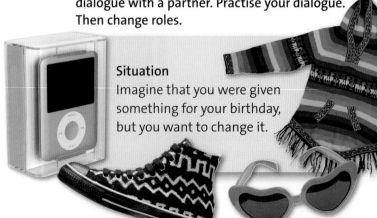

> **Situation**
> Imagine that you were given something for your birthday, but you want to change it.

WRITING ■ A formal letter
I can write a letter of complaint.

1 Read the model text and answer the questions.

  1 Why did the author write this letter?
    a To ask for an explanation.
    b To request compensation.
    c To criticize a product.
  2 Who is the person writing to?
  3 Which paragraph describes the problem?
  4 What happened when the person took the sweatshirt back to the shop?
  5 Study the highlighted sentence in the model text. Why has the author used the passive tense here?

> 5 East Street
> Plimford
> PL2 7LA
> 11th May 2011
>
> The Manager
> Streetwear lcl
> Oval Street
> Oxford
>
> Dear Sir or Madam,
>
> I am writing to complain about a product that I bought from your shop in Oxford.
>
> Two weeks ago, I bought a rather expensive blue hooded sweatshirt. The first time it was washed, the colour came out and all my other clothes were dyed blue. I took it back to the shop yesterday with the receipt, but the assistant was extremely unhelpful. She refused to change it for something else or to give me a refund. I was told that I had not followed the washing instructions. I was really upset because I had read the label carefully. In my opinion, the problem was caused by the bad quality of the sweatshirt.
>
> I would be very grateful if you would refund the price of the sweatshirt. I enclose the receipt. I would also appreciate compensation for the other clothes that were damaged.
>
> I look forward to hearing from you.
>
> Yours faithfully,
>
> J. Stevens

2 Study the key phrases. Put the phrases in the order of the text. Then check your answers.

> **KEY PHRASES ◯ Formal letters**
>
> I am writing to complain about …
> I enclose the receipt.
> Yours faithfully,
> I would be grateful if you would …
> I look forward to hearing from you.

Language point: Adverbs of degree

3 Study the words in blue in the model text. Do they come before nouns or adjectives? Rewrite the sentences with the correct adverbs.

The assistant was rude to me. She walked away when I spoke to her.
(quite / extremely)
The assistant was extremely rude to me.
  1 Those designer jeans cost 800 euros. They're expensive! (very / a bit)
  2 Wow! She looks cool in those jeans. (really / a bit)
  3 The trousers are tight, but they still fit. (a bit / really)
  4 The assistant wasn't helpful. (very / rather)
  5 That jacket is nice, but I prefer the other one. (extremely / quite)

4 **ACTIVATE** Follow the steps in the writing guide.

> **◯ WRITING GUIDE**
>
> **A TASK**
>
> Write a letter of complaint about something you have bought.
>
> **B THINK AND PLAN**
>
> **1** What is the product?
> **2** Where did you buy it?
> **3** How much did it cost?
> **4** What is wrong with it?
> **5** What do you believe the cause is?
> **6** What have you done about it?
> **7** What action are you requesting?
>
> **C WRITE**
>
> **Paragraph 1: The reason for writing**
> *I am writing to complain about …*
> **Paragraph 2: The problem**
> *… I bought … at the store.*
> *The first time …*
> **Paragraph 3: Requested action**
> *I would be grateful if …*
>
> **D CHECK**
>
> • formal language
> • adverbs of degree
> • the passive

Vocabulary

1 Choose the correct words.

1 I like your **hooded** / **baggy** jeans.
2 They **grow** / **manufacture** coffee in Brazil.
3 He's growing a **tattoo** / **beard**.
4 She never wears **lipstick** / **piercings**.
5 90% of the cotton is **exported** / **manufactured** to other countries.
6 Her **piercings** / **sideburns** really suit her.
7 That shirt was **produced** / **supplied** in China.
8 He is a famous clothes **worker** / **designer**.

2 Add prefixes to make the negative of the adjectives in the box. Then complete the sentences with the adjectives.

> organized   legal   fair   respectful
> possible   responsible   common

1 It was ___ to punish him. It was an accident.
2 You shouldn't wear shorts in church. It's ___.
3 You can't find anything. You're so ___.
4 His writing is ___ to read.
5 It's ___ to drive a car without a licence.
6 It's ___ to see people in top hats these days.
7 It was ___ of you to leave your bag in the car.

Language focus

3 Complete the sentences with the correct form of the passive.

1 Our school ___ ten years ago. (build)
2 Cars ___ in twenty years' time. (not use)
3 ___ better next year? (workers / pay)
4 Their products ___ all over the world in the next ten years. (sell)
5 *Hamlet* ___ by Shakespeare. (write)
6 Pesticides ___ by organic cotton growers. (not use)
7 ___ in Britain these days? (grapes / grow)
8 Trousers ___ by women in the 1920s. (not wear)

4 Make the active sentences passive. Include the agent if necessary.

1 Designer shops sell these shoes.
2 We will recycle more rubbish.
3 Someone stole my mobile phone.
4 They make clothes in India.
5 The author didn't sign the novel.
6 People don't speak English here.
7 A lot of fans watched the match.

5 Write questions and answers for the sentences in exercise 4. Use the passive.

Are these shoes sold in designer shops? Yes, they are.

Communication

6 Choose the correct answers.

1 Do you like his hairstyle?
   a No, it doesn't suit him.   b Maybe.
   c It looks like it, yes.
2 She's dyed her hair green!
   a It really suits you.
   b I think it looks cool.
   c It doesn't fit her.
3 Those shoes really suit you.
   a I'll take them then.   b Yes, it suits me.
   c That sounds great.
4 Can I try this on, please?
   a Yes, here it is.   b That's OK.
   c Yes, sure.
5 It isn't too short, is it?
   a I'm sure.   b No, I don't think so.
   c I don't like it.
6 Those piercings look really cool, don't they?
   a Yes, they are.   b No, they look awful!
   c They don't fit him.

Listening

7 ● 2.29   Listen and complete the text.

London is an important fashion capital. The London Fashion Week is held ¹___ a year. At this show, there will be a lot of ²___ of new fashion. This week, nearly ³___ ethical designers will present their clothes in the EstEthica section of the show. Ethical clothes are made of organic or recycled materials to reduce their impact on the ⁴___. The popularity of ethical fashion is ⁵___ and many big labels are now interested. The Fashion Show is only open to journalists and ⁶___ because it is a business event. The general public can visit the London Fashion Weekend and the tickets for this event are sold ⁷___.

1 Look at the webpage. Match links 1–4 with sections A–D.

The Goth scene

1 Attitude **2 Hair and make-up** **3 Clothes and jewellery** **4 Music**

Goth culture developed in the 1980s in Britain from the punk-rock movement. Like the punks, goths are seen by society as rebels. Goths have a very distinctive dark look and they often shock people because of their appearance.

A Goths define themselves by their dark look. The typical goth will only wear black clothing. They also wear a lot of silver jewellery, especially chains and rings. Some goths, like the punks before them, wear huge black boots and have large piercings. Goth fashion aims to shock people and to make them think.

B All goths dye their hair either black or blue or both. A true goth won't leave home without a lot of black make-up. They wear black eyeliner and often black lipstick and nail varnish as well.

C Goths like dark, heavy music with lyrics about horror, magic and death which create a mysterious atmosphere. Goths listen to bands like The Cure and Nine Inch Nails.

D Goth culture is all about attitude. They don't care about what other people think of them. They see society differently and they make up their own minds. Although they look dark and gloomy, a sense of humour is important to most goths. They like to laugh at society and at themselves.

2 Write a webpage about another urban tribe. Follow the steps in the project checklist.

> ☐ **PROJECT CHECKLIST**
>
> **1** Choose an urban tribe. Use one of the ideas below or your own idea.
>
> > emos skaters grungers preppies hippies
>
> **2** Write an introduction to your urban tribe. Include information about its origins and main characteristics. Use the internet to find information, if necessary.
>
> **3** Use headings 1–4 or your own headings to plan the contents of your webpage.
>
> **4** Find photos to illustrate your webpage on the internet or in magazines.

3 Exchange your webpage with the rest of the class.
What is the most popular tribe in the class? Which is the best webpage?

A perfect world

Start thinking

1 How many presidents can you name?
2 What does your country's flag look like?
3 At what age can you vote in your country?

Aims

Communication: I can ...

- talk about permission and obligation.
- understand a text about micronations.
- talk about a future situation and its consequences.
- talk about government policies.
- talk about what I would do in likely or unlikely situations.
- apologize and express regrets.
- write an opinion essay.

Vocabulary

- Nations and government
- Government policies

Language focus

- *make* and *let*
- First conditional + *if* or *unless*
- Second conditional
- First and second conditionals
- Regrets about past and present

English Plus Options

Extra listening and speaking
Doing an interview
⇨ Page 93

Curriculum extra
Language and literature:
Word building: adjectives
⇨ Page 101

Culture
High school elections
⇨ Page 109

Vocabulary bank
Prepositions and nouns;
Protest
⇨ Page 117

VOCABULARY AND LANGUAGE FOCUS
■ Nations and government
I can talk about permission and obligation.

1 Match definitions 1–9 with the words in blue in the *Nations quiz*.

1 A country's money.
2 The rules that everyone in a country must obey.
3 Lines which separate different countries or regions.
4 The heads of different ministries.
5 The process to choose a representative or leader.
6 People who are members of a country and have the nationality of that country.
7 A coloured design that symbolizes a country.
8 A group of people who govern something.
9 The most important representative of a country.

2 Do the *Nations quiz*. Then check your answers with a partner.

Nations quiz

1 How many borders has your country got with other countries?

2 At what age do the laws of your country allow marriage?

3 How many ministers in your country can you name?

4 How many nations are there in the European Union?

5 What is the currency of Japan and what colours and symbol are on its flag?

6 What is the name and title of the head of state in your country?

7 Has the European Union got more citizens than China?

8 Are the majority of politicians in your country's government from the left, right or centre?

9 What is a democracy?

10 When is the next national election in your country? How often are elections held? Do people have to vote in elections?

3 Complete the sentences with the words in the box. Tell your partner which ideas you agree or disagree with. Give your reasons.

> borders laws currencies flag elections
> citizens government ~~democracy~~

1 Most teenagers can't vote, so is this really a **democracy**? Should we let all people over sixteen vote in ___?
2 Our ___ isn't very colourful or interesting. Maybe we could let children design a new one.
3 Many politicians are very old. We should make them leave ___ when they are sixty.
4 Why not let ___ from every country cross our ___ when they like?
5 In my ideal society there aren't any ___ and we let people do anything they want.
6 Why are there different ___? We should make everybody use the same money.

make and *let*

4 Complete the sentences from exercise 3. Then choose the correct options in the rules.

1 Should we ___ teenagers vote in elections?
2 We should ___ politicians leave government when they are sixty.
3 We ___ people do anything they want.
4 We should ___ everybody use the same money.

> **◯ RULES**
>
> 1 We use *let* to express **obligation / permission** and *make* to express **obligation / permission**.
> 2 We use *make* and *let* with an object pronoun or noun + **infinitive / to + infinitive**.

(More practice ⇨ Workbook page 49)

5 🔊 2.35 Listen and complete the sentences with *make* or *let*.

He won't **let** the students go home early.
1 Can you ___ Helen play, please?
2 My dad ___ us watch the film.
3 They ___ all citizens vote in Australia.
4 Did they ___ you and Anna eat the cabbage?
5 John's girlfriend doesn't ___ him watch football if there's a good film on TV.
6 I'm going to ___ the kids clean the kitchen.

6 ACTIVATE Make six sentences with your own ideas. Work in pairs and find out if your partner agrees or disagrees with you.

We Parents Teachers The police Politicians	should shouldn't	make let	children ... people ... the Government ... students ... us ...

(Teachers should let us use mobile phones in class.)

(I don't agree. I think they should make students turn them off.)

> **◯ Finished?**
> Write sentences about what your parents and teachers make or let you do. Do you think it's fair or not?
> Our teacher makes us learn irregular verbs.

1 Look at the title and the photos. What do you think a *micronation* is?

2 🔊 2.36 Read and listen to the text. Write *true* or *false*. Correct the false sentences.

  1 Most micronations do not appear on official maps.

  2 All micronations start online.

  3 Britain doesn't recognize Sealand as a country.

  4 Bergonia only exists on the internet.

  5 The planet Verden is part of the Aerican Empire.

  6 The citizens of the Aerican Empire voted for their emperor in an election.

> **STUDY STRATEGY ○ Guessing meaning from context**
>
> **3** Reading new words in context can help you to guess their meaning. Find the words in blue in the text. What parts of speech are they? Look at the context of each word and match with the correct synonyms 1–5.
>
>   **1** unreal   **2** before   **3** land
>   **4** started   **5** group

4 **BUILD YOUR VOCABULARY** Look again at the text and find prepositions to go with these words. Then write an example sentence for each.

> the internet fun holiday advance
> reality trouble

5 Choose the correct prepositions and answer the questions with your own ideas. Then ask and answer with a partner.

  1 Have you ever done something silly **in** / **on** purpose?

  2 How do you learn things **by** / **with** heart?

  3 Do you think you will have the same friends **for** / **of** life?

  4 Have you ever taken something that wasn't yours **by** / **in** mistake?

  5 Do you always get to lessons **on** / **at** time?

  6 Would you like to work **in** / **at** business when you leave school?

6 **YOUR OPINIONS** Ask and answer the questions.

  1 Which micronation in the text do you think is the most interesting? Why?

  2 What do you think of the people who have started micronations?

  3 What are the good and bad things about your own nation?

  4 Would you like to rule a nation? Why / Why not?

  5 Where would you start a new nation and what would you call it?

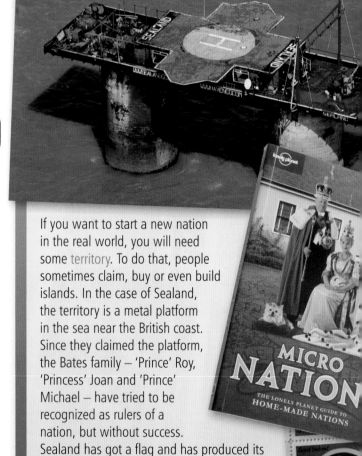

Micronations

If you look for Sealand, Bergonia or the Aerican Empire on a map, you won't find them. People sometimes try to create new countries either in reality or on the internet, but usually they aren't recognized by the UN or the rest of the world. Why create a new country? Well, it seems that there are always people who are unhappy with the government, policies or laws where they live and they want to create a better place. Others simply do it for fun.

If you want to start a new nation in the real world, you will need some territory. To do that, people sometimes claim, buy or even build islands. In the case of Sealand, the territory is a metal platform in the sea near the British coast. Since they claimed the platform, the Bates family – 'Prince' Roy, 'Princess' Joan and 'Prince' Michael – have tried to be recognized as rulers of a nation, but without success. Sealand has got a flag and has produced its own currency and stamps. However, you will be in trouble if you visit without an invitation.

LANGUAGE FOCUS ● **First conditional +** *if* or *unless*
I can talk about a future situation and its consequences.

6

1 Complete sentences 1–4 from the text with the words in the box. Then choose the correct options in the rules.

> should   visit   know   apply   'll be   if
> won't let

1 If you ___ for a Bergonian passport, you'll receive one.
2 You ___ in trouble if you ___ without an invitation.
3 They ___ you land unless they ___ you.
4 You ___ contact them in advance ___ you want to visit.

(More practice ⇨ Workbook page 49)

○ **RULES**

1 We use the first conditional to talk about the results of actions which are **likely or possible** / **unlikely or imaginary**.
2 When *If* + present simple clause is first, there **is** / **isn't** a comma between the two clauses.
3 We **never** / **always** use *will* in the *if* clause.
4 We **can** / **can't** use modal verbs (like *should* or *might*) instead of *will*.
5 *Unless* + affirmative means the same as *if* + **negative** / **affirmative**.

You should contact them in advance if you want to visit. The Bates family won't let you land unless they know who you are. The platform was once invaded by a small gang of people, so visitors are no longer welcome.

Apart from the micronations which have real territory, there are now hundreds of virtual countries on the internet. Bergonia, for example, was started as a hobby by an American lawyer, Joseph Cometti. He has written a complete online history of his fictional country and has invented flags, maps, laws and other documents. If you apply for a Bergonian passport, you'll receive one, but you won't actually be able to travel with it.

Another popular, but less sensible micronation is the Aerican Empire, which was founded in 1987 and has more than a hundred citizens. The nation's website says that it owns a house in Canada, land on Pluto and will also own the planet Verden, if somebody discovers it. It's the ideal nation for people with a sense of humour. Eric Lis declared himself emperor and there are elections for jobs such as Minister of Silly Things. There are also twenty-eight public holidays every year, including Happy Things Day and Idiots' Day. Therefore, if you want to go on holiday all the time, just become an Aerican.

2 Complete the sentences using the correct form of the verbs in brackets.

1 If I ___ your jacket, I ___ you. (find / ring)
2 ___ you ___ with me if I ___ the tickets? (come / buy)
3 I ___ to the party unless you ___ to go. (not go / decide)
4 I ___ this CD unless it ___ in the sale. (not buy / be)
5 If she ___ the election, she ___ the country. (win / change)
6 The minister ___ to you unless you ___ her your email address. (not reply / send)

3 The Wetzian Empire is another micronation. Make rules for the Empire by completing the sentences.

1 The Empire will welcome anyone as a citizen if …
2 The citizens will elect the Emperor unless …
3 The Empire will not start a war unless …
4 Citizens will lose their citizenship if …
5 If you visit the Empire, you should …
6 The Empire will not tax its citizens unless …
7 The Empire will come to an end if …

4 **ACTIVATE** Work in pairs. Ask and answer the questions using the first conditional.

What will you do at the weekend if …

1 it rains?
2 you're bored?
3 you're tired?
4 you get some money?
5 you meet some friends?
6 you can't go out?

(What will you do at the weekend if it rains?)

(If it rains, I'll play video games.)

○ *Finished?*
Rewrite your answers to the questions in exercise 4 using *unless*.
I'll play video games at the weekend unless it rains.

1 Check the meaning of the verbs in the box. Then read policies 1–9 below. Which do you agree with? Which do you disagree with?

> ban   reduce   raise   lower   invest   stand for   introduce   elect   tax   vote   cut   permit

If I was president, I'd ...

1 lower the age that people can <u>leave school</u>.

2 raise the price of <u>petrol</u> and improve <u>public transport</u>.

3 ban <u>violent computer games</u>.

4 cut <u>politicians' salaries</u> and reduce the money spent on <u>the military</u>.

5 build <u>better schools</u>.

6 tax <u>super-rich sports stars</u> and invest more money in <u>sports facilities</u>.

7 permit <u>all people over fifteen</u> to vote and <u>people over sixteen</u> to stand for Parliament.

8 introduce a holiday for each person <u>on their birthday</u>.

9 elect <u>celebrities</u> to the government and not politicians.

2 ● 2.37 Listen to Sophie and Ross talking about what they would do if they were president. Which ideas from exercise 1 do they mention?

3 ● 2.37 Listen again and complete the sentences.
  1 If Sophie was president, she would ___.
  2 People like nurses don't earn ___.
  3 If you taxed footballers more, they'd ___.
  4 If classrooms were more comfortable, people would ___.
  5 If petrol was more expensive, people wouldn't ___.
  6 If Ross was a politician, Sophie would ___.

4 ACTIVATE Work in pairs. Read the policies in exercise 1 again. Replace the <u>underlined</u> words with your own ideas. Then present five of the most important ideas to the class and give your reasons.

LANGUAGE FOCUS ■ Second conditional • First and second conditionals

I can talk about what I would do in likely or unlikely situations.

Second conditional

1 Read the rules. Then complete the table with five of the words and phrases in the box. Do we use the second conditional to talk about possible or imaginary situations?

> ○ **RULES**
>
> 1 We form the second conditional with *if* + past simple and *would / wouldn't* + infinitive.
> 2 We use *if* + past simple to describe the situation and *would / wouldn't* + infinitive to describe the result.
> 3 We form questions with *Would* + infinitive and *if* + past simple.

> would   taxed   they'll go   they'd go   use
> would use   raise   ~~were~~   used   raised

Situation	Result
If you **were** a politician,	I'd vote for you.
If you ¹___ the footballers more,	² ___ to a different country.

Result	Situation
What ³___ you do	if you were president?
People ⁴___ public transport	if we ⁵___ the price of petrol.

(More practice ⊂⊃ Workbook page 51)

2 Choose the correct words.

1 If we **would ban / banned** violent games, people **do / would** still play them.
2 If politicians **played / play** football, would people **think / thought** they were cool?
3 If people **wouldn't / didn't** have cars, they **will / would** be healthier.
4 We **didn't / wouldn't** vote for you if you **stood / would stand** for president.
5 I **would / will** buy a new computer if I **had / would have** more money.
6 She **would / will** stand for the election if she **had / would have** more support.
7 Would you **buy / bought** a big car if you **had / will have** a lot of money?

3 Look again at the ideas in exercise 1 on page 62. Write about the results of each policy. Use the second conditional.

If we lowered the school-leaving age, many young people would stop studying.

First and second conditionals

4 Match examples 1–4 with descriptions a and b. Which conditional is used in each sentence?

1 If I have time, I'll help you.
2 If I had time, I'd help you.
3 He'll win the election if he's honest.
4 He'd win the election if he was honest.

a The speaker thinks that this situation is imaginary or unlikely.
b The speaker thinks that this situation is possible.

(More practice ⊂⊃ Workbook page 51)

5 Write two versions of each sentence, one for person a and one for person b. Use first and second conditionals.

If I **see** a lion, I'll take a photo. (tourist on safari)
If I **saw** a lion, I'd take a photo. (tourist in London)

1 If I ___ (earn) a million euros, I ___ (buy) a Ferrari.
  a you   b famous footballer
2 It ___ (be) brilliant if we ___ (win) the league.
  a manager of good team
  b manager of bad team
3 If I ___ (become) president, I ___ (cut) taxes.
  a your friend   b politician

6 **ACTIVATE** Complete the sentences with your own ideas and the first or second conditional. Then ask and answer with a partner.

1 If I was the mayor of this town, ...
2 If I have time tonight, ...
3 If I pass my exams, ...
4 If I go on holiday next summer, ...
5 If I visited the USA, ...
6 If I won a million euros, ...

(What would you do if you were mayor?)

(I'd build a new sports stadium.)

> ○ *Finished?*
> **Continue the chain of consequences.**
> If I won a million euros, I'd buy a beautiful island in the Pacific. If I had an island, I'd ...

SPEAKING ■ Apologizing and expressing regrets

I can apologize and express regrets.

1 Look at the photo. Where are Dean, Marie and Grace? Do you think Dean looks …

a apologetic? b worried? c angry?

2 ● 2.38 Listen to the dialogue. Why is Dean apologizing?

Marie	What's up, Dean? You look upset. Is something wrong?
Dean	I'm afraid so. I've done something silly. It's the party on Saturday. I said we could have it at my house.
Grace	And now we can't?
Dean	I'm afraid not. My grandparents are coming to stay.
Grace	But didn't you say that your parents were spending the weekend with them?
Dean	I got it wrong. I didn't realize they were coming here. I'm really sorry.
Marie	Oh no! I wish we hadn't sent out the invitations!
Grace	We'll have to do them all again.
Marie	First, we'll have to find somewhere else to have the party. I wish we had a bigger house. Ours is too small.
Grace	I suppose we could have it at my place. My parents probably won't mind and we've got a big garden.
Marie	If I were you, I'd ask your parents before we decide anything.
Grace	OK. I'll phone you both this evening.

3 Study the key phrases. Which phrases express regret? Practise the dialogue with a partner.

> **KEY PHRASES ○ Apologizing and expressing regrets**
>
> Is something wrong?
> I'm afraid so / not.
> I got it wrong.
> I didn't realize …
> I'm really sorry.
> I wish I hadn't …
> If I were you, I'd …

(Pronunciation: Contractions ⟹ Workbook page 91)

Language point: Regrets about past and present

4 Read the rules. Then find examples in the dialogue.

> **RULES ○**
>
> 1 We use *I wish* + past perfect to talk about past regrets.
> 2 We use *I wish* + past simple to talk about present regrets.

(More practice ⟹ Workbook page 51)

5 ● 2.39 Complete the mini-dialogues using the correct form of the verbs in brackets. Then listen and practise the mini-dialogues with your partner.

1 **Ann** Is something wrong?
 Ed Yes. I wish John ¹__ (be) here. We can't win the game without him.
 Ann Oh dear! I forgot to tell him about today's match. I'm really sorry.
 Ed I wish I ²__ (tell) him yesterday.

2 **Jill** I think it's going to snow!
 Alex Oh no! I wish I ³__ (not forget) my coat.
 Jill I wish we ⁴__ (catch) the bus.

6 **ACTIVATE** Work in pairs. Prepare a new dialogue with a partner. Use situation 1. Practise your dialogue. Then change roles and use situation 2.

Situation 1	**Situation 2**
You and your friend want to go to a concert. You forgot to buy the tickets and they've sold out.	Your friend gave you money to buy him / her something in town. You bought the wrong thing.

1 Read the model text and answer the questions.

1 What policy does the writer disagree with?

2 Who would be most affected by the new law? Why?

3 Which paragraph describes the negative effects of the new law?

4 Which paragraph suggests an alternative policy?

5 How does the writer summarize his arguments?

2 Study the key phrases. Which key phrases do not introduce opinions?

> **KEY PHRASES ◯ Opinions**
>
> In my view, ...   It seems to me that ...
> In the first place, ...   In conclusion, ...
> I believe that ...   I feel strongly that ...
> I've no doubt that ...

Changing laws.docx

Changing laws

1 The Government plans to introduce a new law which will mean that young people won't be able to ride scooters or motorbikes unless they are eighteen. In my view, this would have some negative consequences.

2 In the first place, I believe that scooters and motorbikes are necessary because public transport is very limited in some areas. Young people can't always depend on their parents for transport. So if this law is introduced, I've no doubt that a lot of them will have difficulty in travelling from place to place. I also think that this would discriminate against young motorists, who aren't all irresponsible.

3 If the aim of the Government is to lower the number of road accidents, it seems to me that there's a better alternative. If they spent more money on better roads and road signs, transport in this country would be safer.

4 In conclusion, although I realize that we need to improve road safety, I feel strongly that this new law is not the answer.

Language point: References and pronouns

3 Look again at the text. Match the words in blue with a–d.

a the Government

b the new law

c young motorists

d young people

4 **ACTIVATE** Follow the steps in the writing guide.

> **◯ WRITING GUIDE**
>
> **A TASK**
>
> Imagine that the Government in your country plans to shorten the length of the school holidays in order to improve the level of education. Write an opinion essay.
>
> **B THINK AND PLAN**
>
> 1 In general, do you think that this would have positive or negative consequences?
>
> 2 What will be the effects of this law if it is introduced?
>
> 3 Is it fair or unfair? Why?
>
> 4 Is there an alternative method to achieve the Government's aims?
>
> 5 What are the alternative methods and their results?
>
> **C WRITE**
>
> Paragraph 1: Introduction
> *The Government plans to ...*
> Paragraph 2: Argument
> *In the first place, I believe that ...*
> Paragraph 3: Alternative
> *If the aim of the Government is ...*
> Paragraph 4: Conclusion
> *In conclusion, ...*
>
> **D CHECK**
>
> • phrases to introduce opinions
> • references and pronouns
> • first and second conditionals

Vocabulary

1 Complete the text with the words in the box.

> borders currency flag election citizens
> head of state nations democracy

France is a ¹___. The ²___ is an elected president. There is a general ³___ every five years when ⁴___ vote for the president and for members of parliament. France has ⁵___ with six other European ⁶___. The ⁷___ of France is blue, white and red and the ⁸___ is the euro.

2 Complete phrases 1–8 with the words in the box.

> elect lower stand for permit
> introduce raise invest ban

1 ___ a new president
2 ___ violent films
3 ___ Parliament
4 ___ the voting age from 18 to 16
5 ___ in better schools
6 ___ new policies
7 ___ taxes on tobacco
8 ___ young people to ride scooters

Language focus

3 Order the words and write sentences.

1 lets / John's sister / drive / him / her car
2 on weekdays / won't / me / my parents / go out / let
3 citizen / should / they / every / vote / make / ?
4 stay / the teacher / us / after school / made
5 your friend / does / next to / your teacher / sit / you / let / ?
6 take / make / us / didn't / our teacher / a test

4 Complete the sentences using the correct form of the verb in brackets.

1 If you leave early, you ___ on time. (arrive)
2 I ___ unless Dad pays for my ticket. (not go)
3 If someone stole my scooter, I ___ the police. (call)
4 What would you do if you ___ your passport? (lose)
5 If you make dinner, what ___? (you / cook)
6 If I ___ a vote, I'd be more interested in politics. (have)

5 Write past or present regrets for the situations.

I didn't phone John earlier and now he's out.
I wish I'd phoned him earlier.

1 I bought a concert ticket and now I can't go.
2 You've got a mobile phone, but you'd like to have a smart phone.
3 We cycled to school and now it's raining.
4 I'm no good at basketball because I'm not tall.
5 I did badly in the history test because I went out last night.
6 I live in the country, but I'd prefer to live in a big city.

Communication

6 Complete the dialogue with the words in the box.

> so wrong were let wish not

Lucy Is something ¹___, Phil? You look upset.
Phil It's my science project. I ²___ my little brother use my computer and he deleted the file.
Lucy You mean Adam deleted your science project?
Phil I'm afraid ³___. I ⁴___ I hadn't let him use the computer.
Lucy Didn't you make a copy?
Phil I'm afraid ⁵___. I've told Mr Butler. I've got until next Monday to redo it.
Lucy If I ⁶___ you, I'd make Adam do it!

Listening

7 ⊙ 2.40 Listen to people interviewing a politician. Write *true* or *false*.

1 The woman in the interview is the Prime Minister.
2 Her government will cut taxes for everyone.
3 She thinks all citizens should vote by law.
4 Her government would reduce the number of students in classes.
5 A lot of students find jobs in other countries.
6 Her government would consider introducing longer school terms.

Listening

1 Look at the photos and answer the questions.

1 What do the photos show?
2 Why do people do these things?
3 What is the best way for citizens to change things?
4 What protest actions have there been in your country? What were the results?

2 ● 2.41 Listen to a conversation. What are the students unhappy about?

3 ● 2.41 Listen again and complete the sentences.

1 Max didn't see ___ last night.
2 The protests were held ___.
3 More than ___ people participated in the London demonstration.
4 There wasn't a lot of ___ during the protest marches.
5 ___ would like to join the students.
6 Max admires the ___ protestors.

Speaking

4 Work in pairs and prepare a conversation about an issue that you feel strongly about. Discuss possible actions you could take. Answer the questions.

1 What is the issue and why is it a problem?
2 Who will it affect and what will happen?
3 Why do you feel strongly about this issue?
4 What do you want to achieve? Why?
5 What actions are you going to take? Why?

5 Have a conversation. Use your ideas in exercise 4 and the chart below to help you. One of you is A and one of you is B. Change roles.

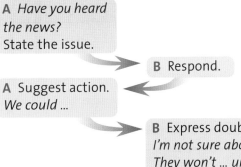

A *Have you heard the news?* State the issue.

B Respond.

A Suggest action. *We could ...*

B Express doubt. *I'm not sure about that. They won't ... unless ...*

A Agree and suggest an alternative action.

B Decide on an action.

Writing

6 Write a short article about an issue you feel strongly about. Describe the consequences if people don't take action. Include information about actions that people are planning and how to support them. Begin like this:

Our town council has decided to ... . We oppose this project because ... . In our view, the environmental / social / economic impact will be ... .

Ups and downs

Start thinking

1 What makes you happy?
2 What are *ups and downs*?
3 What are the Paralympics?

Aims

Communication: I can ...

- compare people and the things they do.
- understand a text about a man who changed his attitude to life.
- talk about imaginary situations in the past.
- understand a discussion about phobias.
- describe things using relative clauses.
- sympathize with someone.
- write about a personal experience.

Vocabulary

- Attributes and personality
- Feelings

Language focus

- Comparing adjectives and adverbs
- Third conditional
- Defining relative clauses
- Non-defining relative clauses

English Plus Options

Extra listening and speaking
Telling an interesting story
⇨ Page 94

Curriculum extra
Biology: The brain
⇨ Page 102

Culture
The British sense of humour
⇨ Page 110

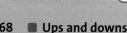

Vocabulary bank
Antonyms;
Expressions with *up* and *down*
⇨ Page 118

VOCABULARY AND LANGUAGE FOCUS
■ Attributes and personality
I can compare people and the things they do.

1 Complete the table with words from the *Ups and Downs* questionnaire. Which adjectives are negative?

Noun	Adjective	Noun	Adjective
success	successful	6___	optimistic
generosity	1___	7___	responsible
2___	passionate	8___	respectful
moodiness	3___	9___	polite
anxiety	4___	10___	confident
pessimism	5___	frustration	11___

2 Complete the sentences with your own ideas using words in exercise 1.

1 I think I'm usually ___.
2 Happy people tend to be ___ and ___.
3 ___ and ___ can make you unhappy.
4 I don't get on with people who are ___ and ___.
5 I admire people who are ___ and ___.
6 ___ and ___ are qualities that I see in older people.
7 ___ and ___ are qualities which are typical of people from my country.

3 Do the *Ups and Downs* questionnaire. Then compare your opinions with a partner. How does your partner cope with life's ups and downs? Choose three adjectives which best describe him / her.

Ups and Downs

How do you cope with life's ups and downs?

1 It's most important to be ...
  a successful.
  b wealthy.
  c generous.

2 In life, it's best not to be ...
  a too honest.
  b too passionate.
  c selfish.

3 Which kind of person is the most difficult?
  a Someone who's often moody and anxious.
  b Someone who's always pessimistic.
  c Someone who's always mean.

4 If someone treats you disrespectfully, what's the best way to react?
  a Politely but firmly.
  b Angrily.
  c In a friendly way.

Comparing adjectives and adverbs

4 Complete the examples and the rules in the table.

Forming adverbs from adjectives	
Rules	**Examples**
Most adjectives: add ¹___	firm → ²___
Adjective ends in -*y*: take off -*y*, add ³___	angry → ⁴___
Adjective ends in -*ic*: add ⁵___	⁶___ → optimistically
Irregular forms	fast → ⁷___ hard → ⁸___ good → well late → late early → early

More practice ⇨ Workbook page 57

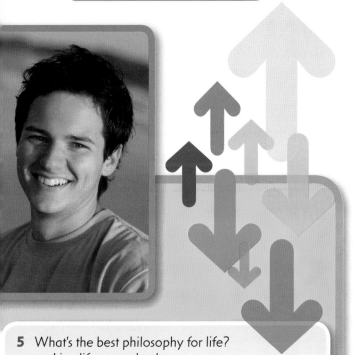

5 What's the best philosophy for life?
  a Live life more slowly.
  b Work hard and play hard.
  c Live fast, die happy.

6 Which pair of attributes best describe your personality?
  a Optimism and passion.
  b Responsibility and respect.
  c Politeness and honesty.

7 What is your attitude when things aren't going well?
  a I stay positive. Things can only get better.
  b I lose confidence. What am I doing wrong?
  c I get frustrated. It's not my fault.

○ *Finished?*
Write a short description of a person you know.

5 Write six sentences describing how you do different things. Use the verbs in the first box and adverbs formed from the adjectives in the second box.

> ~~speak~~ spell play work shout learn behave

> good hard correct ~~polite~~ angry successful responsible careful

I usually speak to my teacher politely.

6 Study sentences 1–5. Which words do we use to form the comparative and superlative forms of adverbs? Complete the table with the words in blue.

Comparatives		Superlatives	
Adjectives	**Adverbs**	**Adjectives**	**Adverbs**
meaner		the most selfish	

  1 He's meaner than anyone I know. He's also the most selfish person I know.
  2 You should take life less seriously and more positively.
  3 We're the least successful team, but we're the most optimistic.
  4 I work more happily at home. It's more comfortable and less stressful.
  5 The richest people gave the least generously and spoke to us the most rudely.

7 Complete the sentences with the comparative or superlative form of an adjective or adverb. Use *more / less* and *the most / the least*.

  1 The person who does the interview ___ will get the job. (successful)
  2 That isn't very positive. Try to think ___. (pessimistic)
  3 Watch out! You should drive ___. (careful)
  4 I like living in a village because it's ___ than the city. (noise)
  5 You need to speak ___ or people won't understand you. (slow)
  6 He always hurts people's feelings. He's ___ person I know. (sensitive)

8 **ACTIVATE** Work in pairs. Take turns describing and guessing people. Use adjectives and adverbs.

> He's the most powerful man in the US.

> President Obama?

1 🔊 3.07 Look at the title of the text and the photos. What do you think the text is about? Choose a or b. Read and listen to the text and check your answer.

a A positive philosophy for life.

b A man asking his girlfriend to marry him.

2 Read the text again and answer the questions.

1 Where did Danny spend his free time after his girlfriend left him?

2 How did he use to communicate with his friends?

3 According to the stranger, what kind of people say 'no'?

4 Why did Danny start his experiment?

5 Why did Danny buy a newspaper?

6 Why did Danny's life change when he bought the newspaper?

7 How long did Danny's experiment last?

3 Complete the summary with six of the words in the box.

> money   pessimistic   interesting
> generous   advice   a beggar   positive
> a stranger   polite

Danny Wallace became ¹___ and depressed after his girlfriend left him. Then one day he met ²___ who gave him some ³___. Danny's new philosophy was to be ⁴___ about everything and more ⁵___ towards other people. As a result, his life became much more ⁶___.

4 BUILD YOUR VOCABULARY Find antonyms in the text for 1–6.

1 accepted (paragraph 1)

2 complicated (paragraph 2)

3 poorer (paragraph 4)

4 meanness (paragraph 4)

5 luckily (paragraph 4)

6 exciting (paragraph 5)

5 Match the words in the box with their antonyms in exercise 3. Then write sentences with the words.

> mean   rude   boring   negative   optimistic

6 YOUR OPINIONS Ask and answer the questions.

1 How often have you said 'no' to something this week? Why?

2 Has anyone ever given you any good advice? Who? What was it?

3 What makes people happiest, in your opinion?

4 How can you help a friend who is unhappy?

5 Do you agree with the writer? What would happen if you always said 'yes'?

THE YES MAN
One little word can change your life …

When his girlfriend left him, Danny Wallace stopped going out and developed a strong relationship with his sofa and remote control. His attitude to everything was negative and his passion for life had gone. He politely refused his friends' invitations and sent 'happy birthday' emails instead of going to parties. He texted people instead of phoning, and phoned people instead of visiting. Danny became the man who always had an excuse.

It was only when a mystery man said three magic words that Danny's whole world started to change and he became more positive and passionate. The stranger, who Danny met on a bus, had a simple philosophy. In his opinion, people without passion always said 'no', so they missed a lot of opportunities in life. His advice to Danny was simple: 'say "yes" more.' The man's philosophy interested Danny and he decided to try an experiment. From that moment, he would always say 'yes'.

So the next time that a friend invited him to play football, Danny said 'yes'. Near his flat, on the way to football, someone was begging for money. The beggar asked for a pound. Danny said 'yes', but he didn't have any change, so he went to the newsagent's, bought a newspaper and then gave the man a pound coin. When a scratch card fell out of the paper, Danny decided to play and he won!

LANGUAGE FOCUS ■ Third conditional
I can talk about imaginary situations in the past.

1 Complete the sentences from the text. Then choose the correct words in the rules.

Situation	Result
If he'd said 'no' to his friend,	he ¹___ stayed at home.
If he'd stayed in,	he ²___ met the beggar.
If he ³___ done the scratch card,	he ⁴___ won the prize.

Result	Situation
Would he have done these things	if he ⁵___ stayed on his sofa?

○ RULES

1 The third conditional describes the imaginary results of **past / future** events which never happened.
2 We form the third conditional with:
If … + **had / have** + past participle (situation) + *would have* + **past participle / past simple** (result).

(More practice ⇨ Workbook page 57)

The prize was £25,000. 'Yes' had suddenly made Danny a wealthier man. If he'd said 'no' to his friend, he'd have stayed at home. If he'd stayed in, he wouldn't have met the beggar, and if he'd said 'no' to the beggar, he wouldn't have bought the newspaper or done the scratch card. And if he hadn't done the scratch card, he wouldn't have won the prize. His optimism and generosity had made a difference. Unfortunately, he lost the £25,000 five minutes later, but that's another story.

It was the beginning of Danny's adventures. In the next six months, he continued to say 'yes' and his life got better and more exciting. As a result, he became a politician and an inventor, met Buddhist monks, travelled to some unusual places, got into some embarrassing situations and met the woman of his dreams! Would he have done these things if he'd stayed on his sofa? So remember … if life is getting dull, just say the magic word.

2 Complete the third conditional sentences.

If you **'d gone** (go) out more, you **'d have made** (make) more friends.

1 Danny ___ (not meet) the man if he ___ (stay) in his flat.
2 Paul ___ (be) happy if he ___ (get) the job.
3 If you ___ (not say) anything, I ___ (not know).
4 ___ we ___ (be) successful if we ___ (work) harder?
5 If you ___ (ask) me politely, I ___ (help) you.
6 ___ Sue ___ (go) to the party if she ___ (know) about it?

3 🔘 3.08 Rewrite the sentences using the third conditional. Include the words in brackets. Then listen and check.

Hayley didn't go because she was tired.
If **Hayley hadn't been tired, she would have gone.** (gone)

1 John didn't go to the party because he felt moody. If ___. (hadn't)
2 The fans respected the captain because he played well. They ___. (wouldn't)
3 I wasn't there, so I didn't see you. I ___. (seen)
4 The team were pessimistic because they lost last week. The team ___. (wouldn't)
5 He gave up smoking when he met his girlfriend. If ___. (hadn't)
6 Sam wasn't optimistic about passing his exams because he hadn't revised much. He ___. (would)
7 She was very successful because she had a positive attitude. If ___. (hadn't)

4 ACTIVATE Ask and answer with a partner.

What would you have done if you …
1 had lived a thousand years ago?
2 hadn't come to school today?
3 had met the US President this morning?
4 had met a film star on the way to school?
5 had found a twenty-euro note in the street?
6 hadn't studied at this school?

○ *Finished?*
Continue the chain of consequences into the past with your own ideas.

Tom wouldn't have broken his leg if he hadn't fallen out of the tree. He wouldn't have fallen out of the tree if …

STUDY STRATEGY ◯ Dictionary skills

1 Look at the dictionary entry and find the abbreviations for the words in the box. Which phrases in the entry are definitions?

> verb   somebody   adjective   noun

> **fright** /fraɪt/ *n* a sudden feeling of fear: *That spider gave me a fright.*
>
> **① frighten** /ˈfraɪtn/ *v* to make sb afraid: *Spiders frighten me.*
>
> **② frightened** /ˈfraɪtənd/ *adj* afraid: *I feel frightened when I see a spider.*
>
> **③ frightening** /ˈfraɪtənɪŋ/ *adj* causing fear: *Spiders are frightening.*

2 Study the example sentences 1–3 in the dictionary entry and match them with a–c. What are two adjective suffixes?

a The adjective refers to the reason for the feeling.

b This is a verb and not an adjective.

c The adjective refers to how you feel.

3 Complete the table. Make adjectives using the verbs in the box. Then use a dictionary to find the nouns.

> ~~bore~~   relax   astonish   embarrass   shock
> fascinate   interest

Verb	-ed adjective	-ing adjective	Noun
bore	bored	boring	boredom

4 🔘 3.09 Listen to a radio programme about phobias. Which of the things in the photos do the speakers mention?

5 🔘 3.09 Listen again and match the speakers, Ben, Jackie and Mary, with descriptions a–d. There is one extra description that you do not need.

a This is a person who used to be terrified of open spaces and crowds.

b This is a person who is scared of heights.

c This is a person who's got a phobia of snakes.

d This is a person who used to be frightened of heights.

6 Choose the correct words in the *All about me* profile. Then write your own answers for 1–10.

7 ACTIVATE Work in pairs. Compare your answers to the *All about me* profile.

> Is there something which terrifies you?

> Yes, I'm terrified of rats.

All about me ...

1 Something which **terrifies / terrifying** me.

2 Something which I'm **worried / worry** about.

3 The most **horrifying / horrified** thing that I've seen or heard this year.

4 A piece of news which **astonished / astonishing** me.

5 A TV programme which I saw recently which I found **fascinated / fascinating**.

6 A celebrity who often **shocking / shocks** people.

7 A singer whose voice is so bad that it's **embarrassed / embarrassing**.

8 Somewhere **interesting / interested** that I've always wanted to visit.

9 The place where I feel most **relaxed / relaxing**.

10 Something people do which I find **annoying / annoyed**.

LANGUAGE FOCUS ● Defining and non-defining relative clauses

I can describe people, things and places using relative clauses.

7

Defining relative clauses

1 Read the rules and find examples for each rule in the *All about me* profile on page 72.

> ### ◯ RULES
>
> 1 We can use the relative pronouns *who*, *which* and *where* when we refer to people, things and places.
> 2 We can use *that* instead of *who* and *which*.
> 3 We can use *whose* for possession.
> 4 We put prepositions at the end of a relative clause.

(More practice ⇨ Workbook page 59)

2 Join the sentence halves with *where, who, whose* and *which*.

1 I know a man …
I know a man who has got weird sideburns.

2 Do you know the village …
3 Can we watch the DVD …
4 Is there a shop in town …
5 These are the boys …
6 Surfing is something …
7 They are the parents …

a you got yesterday?
b I often spend time with.
c has got weird sideburns.
d I can buy a video game?
e child I sometimes look after.
f I'd like to have a go at.
g Dani lives?

3 Make sentences using the phrases in the chart. Then explain your ideas to a partner.

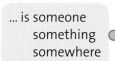 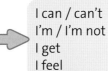

… is someone something somewhere	⇨	who which that	⇨	I can / can't I'm / I'm not I get I feel

⬇

talk to frightened of shocked by	relax with bored with embarrassed by	interested in annoyed with fascinated by

> My brother is someone who I get annoyed with because he spends hours in the bathroom!

Non-defining relative clauses

4 Study the sentences from the listening on page 72. Which is the relative clause in each sentence? Match sentences 1–5 with rules a and b.

1 Wendy Nichols, who is from London University, is a phobia psychologist.
2 You meet people who've had similar problems.
3 I just keep away from places where there are a lot of people.
4 I was supposed to go to Barcelona, where I had a meeting, but I couldn't board the plane.
5 Ben, whose job includes travelling, has a phobia of flying.

> ### ◯ RULES
>
> a A defining relative clause gives important information about the noun. The sentence doesn't make sense without this clause.
> b A non-defining relative clause gives extra information about a noun. The sentence makes sense without this clause. We don't use *that* with these clauses.

5 Combine the two sentences to make one sentence. Use a non-defining relative clause with *who, which, where* and *whose*.

Tom plays basketball brilliantly. He's very tall.
Tom, who's very tall, plays basketball brilliantly.

1 Marc speaks French. His dad comes from Paris.
2 My sister sings in a band. She lives in Dublin.
3 Last summer, I visited Ireland. My father was born there.
4 I can't find my new coat. I bought it last week.
5 My uncle has got a yacht. He's very rich.
6 Jan works for a big company. It makes toys.

6 ACTIVATE Write five sentences about famous people. Then read them to your partner for them to add extra information.

> The Queen of England lives in Buckingham Palace.

> The Queen of England, who has met Lady Gaga, lives in Buckingham Palace.

> ◯ *Finished?*
> **Write definitions for words in this unit. Then ask questions to guess your partner's word.**
> Is it a person who … / a place where … / something which … ?

SPEAKING ◼ Reacting to news and sympathizing

I can sympathize with someone.

1 Look at the photo. How do you think Marie is feeling? Choose the correct answer.

 a terrified **b** fed up **c** excited

2 🔘 3.10 Listen to the dialogue. Is Dean optimistic or pessimistic about Marie's situation?

Dean Hey, Marie, you look a bit down. What's the matter?

Marie Oh, I've just heard that my brother's got a job in Manchester and he's moving away.

Dean Oh, right. Sorry to hear that. It isn't the end of the world though.

Marie I know, but I'll really miss him.

Dean Don't take it too badly. At least he won't be very far away and you can visit him.

Marie That's true, I suppose. But it would have been better if he'd found a job here.

Dean Manchester's a really cool city. You could go up there for weekends.

Marie Yeah, maybe you're right.

Dean Look at it this way; if he hadn't got that job, he'd have been really disappointed.

Marie Yes, I know. It's a fantastic opportunity. He's very excited about it. I mustn't spoil things for him.

Dean Cheer up! Come on. Let's go to a café or something.

Marie OK. Thanks, Dean. I feel a bit better now.

3 🔘 3.11 Complete the key phrases from the dialogue. Listen and check. Then practise the dialogue with a partner.

> **KEY PHRASES ◯ Sympathizing**
>
> You ¹___ a bit down.
> Sorry to ²___ that.
> It isn't the ³___ of the world.
> Don't take it too ⁴___.
> At least ...
> Look at it ⁵___ way.
> Cheer ⁶___!

4 🔘 3.12 Listen. Which words do you hear?

1 At least you **were / weren't** in the same class.
2 She **won't / wouldn't** move to another city.
3 I think he'd **be / have been** happier here.
4 If you **stayed / 'd stayed**, it would be great.
5 I **would / wouldn't** have been happy with her.

> Pronunciation: /θ/, /ð/, /f/ and /v/
> ⇨ Workbook page 92

5 🔘 3.13 Read and listen to the mini-dialogue. What positive aspect does Liz mention? Practise mini-dialogues for situations 1–4 with a partner. Use the key phrases in exercise 3.

Liz You look a bit down. What's the matter?

Shaun I auditioned for a band and they chose another guitar player.

Liz Don't take it too badly. At least you had a new experience.

1 I lost my favourite sweatshirt yesterday.
2 I failed two of my exams.
3 My pet has just died.
4 We aren't going away for a holiday. We're staying here all summer.

6 **ACTIVATE** Work in pairs. Prepare a new dialogue with a partner. Use the situation below. Practise your dialogue. Then change roles.

My best friend is moving to the USA.

I can write about a personal experience.

7

A happy ending

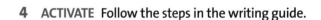

1 This time last year, things weren't going too well for me. I'd failed some exams and I had to take them again. I'd also had a big argument with my best friend, who wasn't talking to me. I was feeling fed up and I wasn't interested in anything. Friends invited me out, but I didn't really want to see them. I spent a lot of time watching DVDs in my room.

2 Everything changed for me the day I saw a TV programme about volunteering. It was about volunteers who were working with athletes who were training for the Paralympic Games. Both the volunteers and athletes were really optimistic and enthusiastic. They made me realize that my problems weren't at all serious and that I should be a bit more positive. I found out that volunteers in my town were working with a Paralympic team too, so I started to go to meetings.

3 These days, I feel much happier. Working as a volunteer has made me feel more useful and sociable. We're helping the athletes to prepare for the next Games, and I aim to go to the Games with the team as a helper. If I hadn't seen the programme, I'd never have had the opportunity.

1 Read the model text and answer the questions.

1 What caused the writer's unhappiness?
2 Which paragraph describes how the writer's life changed?
3 What event changed the writer's life?
4 How did volunteering change the writer's attitude to life?
5 Which paragraph describes how the writer feels now?

2 Study the key phrases. Put the key phrases in the order of the text. Then check your answers.

> **KEY PHRASES ◯ Describing a personal experience**
>
> Things weren't going too well for me.
> If I hadn't … , I'd never have …
> Everything changed for me …
> These days, I feel …
> … made me realize that …

Language point: Modifying comparatives

3 Study the examples. Then order the words in 1–5.

I should be a bit more positive.
I feel much happier.

1 Peter / a lot / more / was / optimistic
2 you / slightly / harder / can / work / ?
3 feeling / I'm / happier / a bit
4 respectfully / please / a little / more / behave
5 life / should / less / stressful / much / be

4 ACTIVATE Follow the steps in the writing guide.

> ◯ **WRITING GUIDE**
>
> **A TASK**
>
> Imagine that you were feeling depressed. Write a story with the title *A happy ending*.
>
> **B THINK AND PLAN**
>
> 1 Things weren't going well for you. Why?
> 2 Things changed suddenly for you. Where were you and what were you doing?
> 3 What did you start to do and why did you like it?
> 4 How did you become happier?
> 5 How do you feel now? Why?
>
> **C WRITE**
>
> **Paragraph 1: In the beginning**
> *This time last year, …*
> **Paragraph 2: How things changed**
> *Everything changed for me the day I …*
> **Paragraph 3: My life now**
> *These days, I feel …*
>
> **D CHECK**
>
> • modifiers
> • relative clauses
> • conditionals

Vocabulary

1 Write the nouns for these adjectives.

1 frustrated ___
2 confident ___
3 polite ___
4 generous ___
5 pessimistic ___
6 moody ___

2 Complete the sentences using a word formed from the word in brackets.

1 Snakes and spiders ___ me. (fright)
2 I feel really ___ at the moment. (bore)
3 Speaking to the class makes me feel ___. (embarrass)
4 I find my younger brother really ___. (annoy)
5 I was ___ when I saw how tall he'd grown. (astonish)
6 My friend was ___ when I told her the story. (shock)
7 Watching TV after school is quite ___. (relax)
8 That TV documentary on Channel 4 was ___. (fascinate)

Language focus

3 Choose the correct words.

1 She sang more **beautifully / beautiful** than ever.
2 The people who work **less hard / the hardest** are usually the most **successful / successfully**.
3 The children played **noisy / noisily** while their parents were chatting **happy / happily**.
4 I'm less **optimistic / optimistically** these days.
5 The boy loves football more **passionate / passionately** than anything else.
6 He did **good / well** in the exam. He got the **better / best** results.

4 Complete the third conditional sentences with the correct form of the verbs.

1 He ___ (train) harder if he ___ (know) how good the other team was.
2 If I ___ (not / tidy) my room, I ___ (not / find) the library book.
3 If I ___ (not be) so tired, I ___ (go) out.
4 ___ (you / work) harder if your parents ___ (send) you to private school?
5 If he ___ (tell) the truth, his mum ___ (not be) so angry.
6 What language ___ (you / chose) if you ___ (not take) English?

5 Complete the sentences with *who*, *which*, *where* or *whose*.

1 I'm not sure ___ pen this is.
2 Is that the shop ___ Tom works?
3 The police officer, ___ loved animals, returned the lost dog to its owner.
4 Football is a sport ___ I find really boring.
5 That's the boy ___ skateboard was stolen.
6 Do you know the guy ___ is singing?
7 I visited Bratislava, ___ I was born.
8 That's a machine ___ makes ice cream.

Communication

6 Complete the mini-dialogue with the phrases in the box.

I suppose   fed up   I know
the end of the world   too badly
What's the matter?

Sally You look ¹___, Josh. ²___

Josh I failed my driving test.

Sally Oh, sorry to hear that. It isn't ³___ though.

Josh ⁴___, but life would be much easier if I could drive.

Sally Don't take it ⁵___. At least you can take the test again.

Josh Yeah, That's true, ⁶___.

Listening

7 🔊 3.14 Listen to four people talking about happiness. Match speakers 1–4 with sentences a–e. There is one extra sentence that you do not need.

Speaker 1 ___   Speaker 3 ___
Speaker 2 ___   Speaker 4 ___

a I think that sort of behaviour is irresponsible.
b Some people are incredibly generous.
c Money doesn't always make people happy.
d Optimistic people tend to be happy.
e People who are moody are no fun to be with.

1 Read the rules and play the personality game.

FEELINGS ???
How well do you know your classmates?

Rules

1 Play the game in groups of four.

2 Pick a situation card and read it to the rest of your group – 'the guessers'.

3 The guessers decide what they think you would do in that situation and how you would feel. They write their answers and you write yours.

4 Each guesser reads their answer, e.g. *I think that Jacob would … . He's an optimistic person so he would(n't) feel …*

5 Read your answer. Any person who guessed your answer scores five points.

6 Repeat the process until everyone has picked a situation card.

7 The winner is the person with the highest score.

A close friend has asked you to lend him / her some money to buy his / her mum a birthday present. He / She can't pay you back for a week or two. You need the cash to buy a new DVD that's just come out. **What would you do and how would you feel?**

Your friends have got together and bought you a bungee jump ticket for your birthday present. They really think that it's something you've always wanted to try. **What would you do and how would you feel?**

You arrive at a party. You don't know many people and you are wearing an old T-shirt and jeans. You suddenly realize that everyone is looking at you. All the other guests are dressed in smart clothes. **What would you do and how would you feel?**

You've been looking forward to a camping trip at the seaside next weekend. You've already booked a boat trip to an island. On Saturday morning, it's raining when you wake up. **What would you do and how would you feel?**

2 Make a personality game. Follow the steps in the project checklist.

> ## ○ PROJECT CHECKLIST
>
> **1** To make your situation cards, first choose four personality attributes you want to test, e.g. *optimism, confidence, generosity, responsibility, honesty*, etc., and then think of four situations which could test these attributes. Choose situations which could create strong feelings.
>
> **2** Cut a piece of paper into four cards.
>
> **3** Write each situation on a different card.

3 Play a new personality game in groups of four. Make a note of your score. Who knows the people in your group the best?

Honestly!

Start thinking

1 What is a *white lie*?
2 What is a *conman*?
3 Where is the Statue of Liberty?

Aims

Communication: I can ...

- request something and report someone's request.
- understand a text about honesty.
- report things that people have said.
- understand a radio programme about famous conmen.
- ask and respond to indirect questions.
- explain and clarify a situation.
- write a narrative with dialogue.

Vocabulary

- Morals
- Reporting verbs

Language focus

- Indirect requests
- Reported speech: tense changes
- Reported and indirect questions

English Plus Options

Extra listening and speaking
Dealing with money
⟶ Page 95

Curriculum extra
Civic and ethical education: Moral values
⟶ Page 103

Culture
Boot camps in the USA
⟶ Page 111

Vocabulary bank
Collocations with *make* and *do*;
Honesty and morals
⟶ Page 119

VOCABULARY AND LANGUAGE FOCUS
■ Morals
I can request something and report someone's request.

1 Complete phrases 1–11. Then check your answers in the *Right or Wrong?* survey.

> hurt keep do pretend ~~break~~ break get feel make (x2) tell (x2)

break a promise
1 ___ something wrong
2 ___ quiet about something
3 ___ the law
4 ___ guilty about something
5 ___ a lie
6 ___ to do something
7 ___ something up
8 ___ around a problem
9 ___ an excuse
10 ___ the truth
11 ___ someone's feelings

2 Work in pairs. Ask and answer using the phrases in exercise 1.

> Do you usually ... ?   Would you ... ?   Have you ever ... ?

> Have you ever broken a promise?

> Yes, I have. Last week, I promised to visit my gran, but I didn't go.

3 🔊 3.19 Read and listen to the *Right or Wrong?* survey. Then work in pairs and exchange opinions about the situations.

> I think Mike was wrong in number 1. I would have told the assistant.

Were the people right or wrong in each of these situations? What would you have done?

1 Mike was buying a computer game in a supermarket. The assistant made a mistake and gave Mike too much change. Mike didn't say anything, but later he felt that he had done something wrong and he gave the money to charity.

2 It was Layla's birthday, but she was shy and didn't want a party or a lot of fuss. She told her brother not to say anything about her birthday and he promised to keep quiet about it. But then he broke his promise and told some of her friends because he didn't think that his sister would mind.

3 John was riding his motorbike at sixty-five kilometres an hour in a fifty kilometres-an-hour zone. He knew that he was breaking the law, but he didn't feel guilty about it. In his opinion, the speed limit was too low and there was no danger. Unfortunately, a police officer stopped him.

Indirect requests

4 Complete the sentences from the survey. Do we use *tell* or *ask* for reporting an order? How do we report negative requests?

Subject + ask / tell	Object	(not) to + infinitive	Other words
She **told**	her brother	¹___ to say	anything.
She ²___	him	³___	his room.
She ⁴___	⁵___	to stop	chatting online.

(More practice ⇒ Workbook page 65)

5 Choose the correct words.

1 They told **she / her** not to leave.
2 I asked her **don't / not** to tell anyone.
3 The teacher **said / asked** us to be quiet.
4 We asked her **give us / not to give us** any homework.
5 My dad asked **we / us** to clean the car.
6 The police officer told the cyclist **wear / to wear** a helmet.

WRONG

4 Stefan's mum asked him to tidy his room, but he didn't do it. When she asked him later, he told a lie and said that he'd done it, because he didn't want an argument. He then decided to tidy his room later in the day.

5 Cathy was on the internet. She pretended to be a different person in a chat room and made up a new identity. She 'became' a nineteen-year-old American girl called Amber. Her mother was concerned and she told her to stop chatting online.

6 Callum bought his sister a scarf for her birthday. She didn't like the colours or the style of the scarf, but she pretended to be very happy with the present. When her brother asked her why she wasn't wearing it, she got around the problem by making an excuse.

7 Jess dyed her hair pink and asked her friend Lauren what she thought of it. Lauren thought that it was awful and decided to tell the truth. But she really hurt Jess's feelings.

6 Rewrite the sentences to make indirect requests.

The criminal told his friend, 'Keep quiet about the robbery.'
The criminal told his friend to keep quiet about the robbery.

1 'Don't break the law again,' the police officers told them.
2 'Don't feel guilty,' I told myself.
3 'Wash the dishes when you've finished,' Mum asked us.
4 He told his girlfriend, 'Stop laughing!'
5 'Walk a bit faster!' you asked me.
6 'Meet me later,' I asked my friend.

7 🔘 3.20 Listen to five dialogues and report what the people have requested. Then listen again and check.

Layla
Layla asked her brother not to tell her friends about her birthday.

1 a police officer   3 Cathy's mum
2 Stefan's mum   4 Jess

8 ACTIVATE Work in pairs. Study the key phrases and situations 1–6. Take turns to make requests. Then report your partner's requests to the class.

KEY PHRASES ◯ Requests

Could you …
Can you …
It would be great if you could …
Would you mind (not) …-ing?

┌──────────────────────┐ ┌──────────────────────┐
│ I'm cold. Can you   │ │ Anna asked me to   │
│ close the window?   │ │ close the window.   │
└──────────────────────┘ └──────────────────────┘

1 I'm cold.
2 I don't understand my homework.
3 I've missed the bus into town.
4 I haven't got any money and I want to go out.
5 The phone's ringing.
6 I can't reach something on the shelf.

◯ Finished?
Write requests that your parents and friends have made this week.
My mum asked me to do the washing-up.

1 Look at the photos and the title of the text. Which of the topics 1–4 do you think the text mentions? Read the text and check your answers.

1 Hurting someone's feelings.
2 Cheating in an exam.
3 Downloading music.
4 Keeping money that isn't ours.

2 **3.21** Read the text again and complete gaps 1–4 with sentences a–e. There is one extra sentence that you do not need. Then listen to the text and check your answers.

a So are older people less honest, or more thoughtful?
b Telling the truth in some situations is considered to be rude.
c In the same way, most people thought that it was OK to buy copied DVDs at a market.
d For young people, it depends on the type of shop.
e They said that it was acceptable to take money from a supermarket because they were very rich.

3 **BUILD YOUR VOCABULARY** Complete the phrases with *make* or *do*. Then check your answers in the text.

1 ___ a survey
2 ___ a difference
3 ___ excuses
4 ___ your best
5 ___ the right thing

4 Complete the sentences with the correct form of *make* or *do*.

1 Have you ___ the washing-up yet?
2 I'm going to ___ a sandwich in a minute.
3 What job do you want to ___?
4 I haven't ___ any plans for the summer.
5 You should ___ a habit of doing exercise every day.
6 Can you ___ me a favour, please?

5 **YOUR OPINIONS** Ask and answer the questions.

1 If you were given too much change in a supermarket, what would you do?
2 How do you feel about copying music illegally?
3 When did you last tell a white lie?
4 Is it always possible to be honest? Why / Why not?
5 Do you think most people are honest?

How honest are we really?

Surprise, surprise, we aren't all perfect! A popular magazine recently published a survey about honesty. Virtually everyone who did the survey admitted that they had been dishonest at some time in their lives. But people had very different ideas about what was acceptable in different situations.

One classic test of honesty is when we're given too much change in a shop. In the survey, 67% of people said that they would return the money, but others said that the answer depended on the shop assistant and the type of shop. Some said, for example, that they would return the money to a small shop, but not to a supermarket, unless the assistant had been very kind. **1**___ They thought that it wouldn't make a difference to a big company.

There was a similar attitude towards software and music: 45% of the people in the survey said that they had already downloaded software or music illegally. They said that this was OK because the companies which sell the software or music 'have got enough money already'. **2**___ It seems that we make excuses for our dishonesty so that we don't feel too guilty.

We also persuade ourselves that it's OK to lie, and we tell 'white lies' when we don't want to hurt people's feelings. **3**___ So if someone asks, 'How do I look?' and they look terrible, what do you say? In that type of situation, it's often kinder to be dishonest. Most people said that they couldn't tell the truth. They'd say that the person looked good. Or if you see your friend's partner with someone else, do you tell your friend? The survey showed very different results for younger and older people: 55% of young people said that they would tell the friend, while only 18% of people over fifty said the same thing. **4**___ The answer isn't clear.

Obviously we should all do our best to be honest, but the survey showed that we don't always do the right thing. Unfortunately, for a lot of people, what's right and wrong isn't always black and white.

I can report things that people have said.

1 Study sentences 1–5. Find these sentences in reported speech in the text. How do the verbs change? Choose the correct words in the rules.

1 'We'll return the money.'
2 'It's acceptable to take money from a supermarket.'
3 'We've already downloaded music.'
4 'We can't tell the truth.'
5 'You look good.'

(More practice ⇨ Workbook page 65)

◯ RULES

When you change direct to reported speech:
1 Verbs in the present simple change to the **future / past simple**.
2 Verbs in the past simple change to the **present perfect / past perfect**.
3 Verbs in the present perfect change to the **past perfect / past simple**.
4 We change *can* to *could*, *will* to *would* and *must* to **had to / have to**.
5 The pronouns and possessive adjectives usually change, e.g.
'I like your hair,' Mark said.
Mark said that he liked my hair.

2 Read the dialogue and complete the summary with the correct pronouns.

Jane I want to meet your friend.
Pete I'll introduce you to him.
Jane I saw him at a party with Liz. We both liked him.

Jane told Pete that she wanted to meet ¹___ friend. Pete said that ²___ would introduce ³___ to ⁴___. Jane said that ⁵___ had seen ⁶___ at a party with Liz and that ⁷___ had both liked ⁸___.

3 Rewrite the sentences using reported speech.

Mary: 'I've never told a lie.'
Mary said that she'd never told a lie.
1 The man: 'I don't feel guilty.'
2 My brother: 'You're making a big mistake.'
3 Phil's father: 'Phil must stay at home.'
4 John: 'I'll keep quiet about the crime.'
5 The children: 'Our teacher can be quite strict.'
6 The teacher: 'Some students didn't do much revision.'
7 His friends: 'We've already seen that film.'

4 ACTIVATE Work in pairs. Take turns making true and false reported statements. Guess the true statements.

(Bill told me that he'd bought a new bike.)

(I don't think that's true. Bill hasn't got a bike.)

◯ *Finished?*
Write five things people have said to you today.
Tania said that she was going shopping after school.

1 Check the meaning of the verbs in the box. Then choose the correct words in the text.

> invite   order   refuse   explain   convince
> offer   agree   complain   admit   insist

FOR SALE: THE EIFFEL TOWER

Tuesday 19.30	Channel 6

In 1925, a conman called Victor Lustig ¹**invited / refused** businessmen to attend a meeting, where he ²**admitted / offered** to sell the Eiffel Tower to them. Lustig didn't own the tower, but he ³**complained / explained** that he represented the city of Paris. It was a lie. He told the businessmen that the city council didn't want the tower, but ⁴**refused / insisted** that it was a secret because the people of Paris would ⁵**complain / order** if they knew about the plans. In the end, a man called Poisson ⁶**agreed / admitted** to buy the tower.

This week's programme tells the story of Victor Lustig and other conmen who have ⁷**convinced / agreed** people to buy some of the world's most famous buildings.

2 Study the verb patterns in the table. Add five more verbs from the text in exercise 1 to the table.

Verb + object + infinitive	
order ask tell invite ¹___	someone to do something
Verb + infinitive	
refuse ²___ ³___	to do something
Verb + that	
complain admit ⁴___ ⁵___	that ...

3 🔊 3.22 Rewrite sentences 1–6. Then listen and check your answers.

'Yes, I lied.' (He admitted ...)
He admitted that he'd lied.
1 'Go to your room, Sandra!' (He ordered ...)
2 'No, I won't go!' (He refused ...)
3 'Shall I open the window?' (She offered ...)
4 'Will you all come to my party?' (He invited ...)
5 'We haven't got any money.' (They complained ...)
6 'I didn't do it!' (He insisted ...)

4 🔊 3.23 Listen to the radio programme. Who was George C. Parker? What happened to him?

5 🔊 3.23 Listen again and write *true* or *false*. Correct the false sentences.

1 Poisson's wife had some doubts about the deal.
2 Poisson didn't complain to the police because he was happy with the deal.
3 George C. Parker told visitors to New York that he owned buildings in the city.
4 Parker had authentic documents for the buildings.
5 Parker sold the Brooklyn Bridge twice.
6 The other prisoners didn't respect Parker.

6 ACTIVATE Work in pairs. Invent a new crime story using verbs in exercise 1. Then present your stories to the rest of the class.

LANGUAGE FOCUS ■ Reported and indirect questions
I can ask and respond to indirect questions.

8

1 Study the direct and reported questions from the listening on page 82. Then write *true* or *false* for 1–4.

> **Direct questions**
>
> **a** 'Why is everything so secret?'
> **b** 'Have you got any documents?'
> **c** 'How did you trick so many people?'

> **Reported questions**
>
> **a** She asked him why everything was so secret.
> **b** They asked if / whether he had any documents.
> **c** They asked Parker how he had tricked so many people.

1 The word order is the same in direct and reported questions.
2 Reported questions have question marks.
3 The tense changes in reported questions.
4 We can use *if* or *whether* in reported yes / no questions.

(More practice ⟹ Workbook page 67)

2 Choose the correct words.

I met a man in London who asked me …
1 whether I **knew / know** where Big Ben was.
2 if I **have / had** been there before.
3 what **did I think / I thought** of the city.
4 where **did I come / I came** from.
5 how much money I **have got / had**.
6 whether I **want / wanted** to buy a souvenir.

3 Rewrite the direct questions as reported questions.

We → John: 'Have you ever broken the law?'
We asked John if he had ever broken the law.
1 Piers → Maya: 'When did you lose your bag?'
2 A man → us: 'Is the bank near the station?'
3 The police officer → me: 'Did you see the thief?'
4 I → my friend: 'Can I borrow €2?'
5 Sarah → Chris: 'Who's the police officer talking to?'
6 The teacher → the students: 'Have you heard about the robbery?'

4 Write six questions. Then work in pairs and report your partner's questions.

> What's the date?

> You asked me what the date was.

5 Study the examples. Does the tense of the verb change in indirect questions? Is it more polite to ask a direct or an indirect question?

Direct questions
'Where is the church?'
Reported questions
She asked where the church was.
Indirect questions
'I'd like to know where the church is.'

(More practice ⟹ Workbook page 67)

6 Write indirect questions using the phrases in the box. Then ask and answer with your own ideas.

> Can you tell me … ?   I'd like to know …
> I was wondering …

1 Will I pass my English exam this year?
2 When does the summer holiday start?
3 Are you staying at this school next year?
4 What's the best place to go on holiday?
5 Is there anything good on TV tonight?
6 What interesting films are on at the cinema?

> I was wondering if I'll pass my English exam this year.

> I'm sure you'll pass.

7 ACTIVATE Work in pairs. Imagine that you are a tourist in New York asking for information. Take turns asking and answering using indirect questions. Use the phrases in exercise 6, and the ideas below or your own ideas.

Central Park / near here
change money / any bank
how / get to Brooklyn
when / Metropolitan Museum / open
how far / Central Station
Chinatown / a good place for shopping

> Can you tell me if Central Park is near here?

> Yes, it's only about ten minutes away.

○ *Finished?*
**Write your partner's responses in exercise 7.
Use different reporting verbs.**

SPEAKING ○ Explaining and clarifying situations

I can explain and clarify a situation.

1 Look at the photo. Do you think Marie is pleased to see Dean?

2 ● 3.24 Listen to the dialogue. Why is Marie upset? Does Marie believe Dean in the end?

Marie	Hi, Dean. How was your weekend?
Dean	Not bad, thanks. Why do you ask?
Marie	Because you told me that you were staying in on Saturday night, but I heard that you were at a party.
Dean	Who told you that?
Marie	Grace said that she'd seen you. How come you didn't tell me about it?
Dean	'Cause I was only there for an hour. I chatted to Paul for a while and then I left.
Marie	But why did you go at all?
Dean	I was only taking my sister. My dad asked me to because he was busy.
Marie	Are you telling me the truth, Dean?
Dean	Honestly, it's true! I wouldn't tell you a lie. If you don't believe me, you can ask Grace.
Marie	OK, OK. I believe you. Sorry, Dean.
Dean	That's OK.

3 Study the key phrases. Which sentence is in reported speech? Practise the dialogue with a partner.

> **KEY PHRASES ○ Explaining and clarifying**
>
> Why do you ask?
> You told me that … , but I heard that …
> How come you didn't tell me about it?
> I was only (taking) …
> Are you telling me the truth?
> Honestly, it's true!
> If you don't believe me, you can …

> Pronunciation: Sentence stress
> ⇨ Workbook page 92

4 ● 3.25 Complete the mini-dialogues with the key phrases in exercise 3. Listen and check. Then practise with a partner.

1

Dan	I hear that you were at Callum's after school.
Viv	I went to get my maths book. I was only there five minutes. ___ ask my sister.
Dan	OK, OK. I believe you. Sorry.

2

Sal	Where were you on Saturday night?
Kev	___ ?
Sal	You told me that you were staying in, but I heard that you were in town.

3

Ruth	We went to see a great band at the Zenith on Saturday.
Andy	___ ?
Ruth	Sorry. I didn't think you'd want to go.

5 **ACTIVATE** Prepare a new dialogue with a partner. Use situation 1. Practise your dialogue. Then change roles and use situation 2.

> **Situation 1**
> You told your parents that you were going to a friend's house for the afternoon to study, but a neighbour saw you in town. The reason you were in town was that you needed a book from the library.

> **Situation 2**
> You told your friend that you were going to see a film on Saturday. He / She went to the cinema and you didn't turn up. The reason you didn't go was that you were ill in bed.

WRITING ■ A narrative
I can write a narrative with dialogue.

8

1 Read the model text and answer the questions.

1 What did the writer do?
2 Who didn't tell the truth?
3 What did the gardener do about the accident? Why?
4 How many people speak in the story?
5 How do you know which parts of the story are dialogue?

2 Study the key phrases. Put them in the order of the text. Then read the model text again and check your answers.

> ### KEY PHRASES ⭘ Telling a story
>
> We were (having a great time) when ...
> To cut a long story short, ...
> In the end, ...
> At first ...
> Just then, ...
> Something happened ...

AN ACCIDENT

1 Something happened a couple of weeks ago which was a real test of my honesty. I was with some friends and we were playing football in a park near town. We were having a great time when I did something rather stupid.

2 There's a statue in the park and, to cut a long story short, I broke the statue's head with the football. We felt bad about the accident and we weren't sure what to do. Just then one of the gardeners suddenly appeared.

'Who broke the statue, lads?' he asked. 'Did you see anything?' At first nobody said anything. We just looked at each other guiltily, then my friend spoke. 'I'm not sure what happened,' he said.

3 He wasn't exactly telling the truth and I knew that I had to say something. 'The ball hit the statue,' I said. 'It was me who broke it.' Surprisingly, the gardener didn't look too upset. 'Well, I'm glad that you admitted it,' he said, 'because I knew it was you. I saw you.'

4 In the end, nothing happened about the statue. The gardener was very good about it and it was an accident after all. It wasn't a pleasant experience, but at least I felt that I'd done the right thing.

Language point: Punctuation in dialogues

3 Study the sentences from the text. Then rewrite sentences 1–6 including commas, question marks, full stops and speech marks.

'Who broke the statue, lads?' he asked.
'I'm not sure what happened,' he said.
'The ball hit the statue,' I said.

1 I'm going home now I said
2 Why did you say that my friend asked
3 I didn't see what happened I told him
4 Are you feeling guilty she asked
5 Who found it the police officer asked
6 You weren't breaking the law he told us

4 **ACTIVATE** Follow the steps in the writing guide.

> ### ⭘ WRITING GUIDE
>
> **A TASK**
>
> Imagine that you were with a friend when you found a wallet with €1,000 inside it. Write a narrative to explain what happened. Include the conversation which you had with your friend.
>
> **B THINK AND PLAN**
>
> 1 Who were you with and what were you doing when you found the wallet?
> 2 How did you feel and what did you say to each other?
> 3 What happened after that?
> 4 Did you tell anybody about your actions? What did they say?
> 5 How did you feel about the experience in the end?
>
> **C WRITE**
>
> Paragraph 1: Introduction – the situation
> *Something happened ...*
> Paragraph 2: Action – what happened?
> *We were ... when ...*
> Paragraph 3: Action – what happened next and what people said
> *Just then, ...*
> Paragraph 4: Conclusion – what happened in the end and how people felt
> *In the end, ...*
>
> **D CHECK**
>
> • punctuation in dialogues
> • past tenses
> • time connectors

Vocabulary

1 Complete the sentences with the verbs in the box.

> tell   hurt   make   feel   keep   pretend
> break   do

1 Why did you ___ your promise?
2 She really ___ my feelings.
3 You should always ___ the truth.
4 You shouldn't ___ guilty. It wasn't your fault.
5 I wish they'd ___ quiet.
6 My mum is very strict – if I ___ something wrong she stops my pocket money.
7 Giles doesn't ___ a good excuse when he forgets his homework.
8 Don't ___ to be happy if you aren't.

2 Complete the sentences with the correct form of *make* or *do*.

1 She asked me to ___ her a favour.
2 I'm going to ___ sandwiches for lunch.
3 Are you sure you are ___ the right thing?
4 He always ___ the washing-up.
5 I haven't ___ any plans for the weekend yet.
6 Please don't ___ a habit of being late.

3 Choose the correct words.

1 The police officer **ordered** / **refused** the driver to get out of his car.
2 He **complained** / **admitted** that he had taken the wallet.
3 I **invited** / **ordered** her to join us for a coffee.
4 He **insisted** / **convinced** me that he wasn't lying.
5 They **refused** / **agreed** to help me, so I did it myself.
6 She **explained** / **convinced** that she had missed the bus.

Language focus

4 Complete the reported sentences with the correct form of the verbs in brackets.

1 He asked her ___ with him. (go out)
2 Tom told me that he ___ Amy recently. (not see)
3 She asked us if we ___ on holiday next week. (go)
4 After the race, I asked her if she ___ tired. (be)
5 Ted told me that his brother ___ his feelings last night. (hurt)
6 Dad told us that he ___ a new car yesterday. (buy)

5 Rewrite the sentences in reported speech.

1 'I like chocolate.' She said that ___.
2 'Can you ride a scooter?' He asked me if ___.
3 'Have you done the exercise yet?' The teacher asked us if we ___.
4 'Clare isn't lying.' Mum said that Clare ___.
5 'I can't swim.' He told me that ___.
6 'Why are you late?' My friend asked me ___.
7 'You must arrive on time.' The coach told us that we ___.

Communication

6 Choose the correct answers.

1 It would be great if you could clear the table.
   a I don't agree.   b Why do you ask?
   c OK, I'll do it right away.
2 Would you mind not saying anything?
   a No, I wouldn't.   b OK. I'll keep quiet.
   c I don't mind.
3 I was wondering if you've seen Phil.
   a No, I haven't.   b Yes, OK.
   c I'm meeting him in town.
4 I heard you went to a party last night.
   a Honestly, it's true.
   b Who told you that?
   c Are you telling the truth?
5 Could you tell me where the post office is?
   a Why do you ask?   b That's OK.
   c Yes, it's in West Street.
6 How come you didn't tell me about the party?
   a But I heard that you were at a party.
   b If you don't believe me, ask Ted.
   c Because I was only there for an hour.

Listening

7 ⏺ 3.26 **Listen and choose the correct words.**

1 Luke thinks Suzy's hair looks **cool** / **terrible**.
2 A woman damaged another car and **didn't admit** / **admitted** it.
3 **Luke** / **Suzy** doesn't think it's dishonest to pick apples in the countryside.
4 Luke has had the phone for **a week** / **a fortnight**.
5 Luke doesn't feel **guilty** / **dishonest** because he kept the mobile phone.
6 Suzy doesn't think it's **right** / **wrong** to download music for free.

Listening

1 Look at the photos and answer the questions.

1 What is each person doing wrong?
2 Which of these actions is the most / least serious?
3 Have you ever done or seen someone do any of these things?
4 What would you do if you saw someone do these things?

2 ● 3.27 Listen to a conversation. What has happened to Tessa?

3 ● 3.27 Listen again and complete the sentences.

1 Tessa was ___ when she realized she had lost her bag.
2 There was ___ in the bag.
3 ___ wouldn't have kept the bag.
4 Tessa decides to phone the ___.
5 Tessa is happy because she's had some good ___.
6 Tessa lost her bag on the way to the ___.
7 A woman found her bag when she was ___.

Speaking

4 Work in pairs and prepare a conversation. Imagine you have lost your bag or wallet and you are telling a friend. Answer the questions.

1 What have you lost and what important things were in it?
2 Where do you think you might have lost it?
3 How do you feel?
4 What have you done about it?
5 What else can you do?

5 Have a conversation. Use your ideas in exercise 4 and the chart below to help you. One of you is A and one of you is B. Change roles.

A You look a bit down. What's the matter?

B I've lost my …

A Sympathize. I'm sorry to hear that. It isn't the end of the world.

B Respond. I know, but I had … and … in it.

A Where do you think you might have lost it?

B I'm not sure. It might have been … I only realized I'd lost it …

A Make a suggestion. If I were you, I'd …

B Respond. You might be right. I wish I'd …

Writing

6 Write a letter to a friend telling him / her about something you lost and found again. Explain how it happened, what you did and what happened in the end. Begin like this:

Hi,
How are you? I've had an unpleasant experience. I was … . When I got … I realized that … .

EXTRA LISTENING AND SPEAKING ▪ Talking about a family likeness

I can talk about someone I take after.

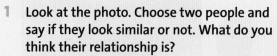

1

1 **Look at the photo. Choose two people and say if they look similar or not. What do you think their relationship is?**

They've got the same …
They've got different …
I think they're … and …

2 ● 1.14 **Listen to a conversation between Michael and Melissa. Which members of Michael's family do they mention?**

3 ● 1.14 **Study the key phrases. Then listen again and choose the correct answers (1–6).**

> **KEY PHRASES** ○ **Talking about a family likeness**
>
> You (don't) look like …
> We've got similar / the same …
> You don't look anything like him.
> Neither of us has / is …
> He's / She's like me in other ways.
> Who do you take after?

1 Who did Melissa see when she arrived?
 a Michael, then Ed.
 b Michael's mum, then Michael.
 c Ed, then Michael.
2 How are Michael and Ed similar?
 a They've got the same colour hair.
 b Their personality is similar.
 c They're both tall.
3 Which is true?
 a Melissa does a lot of sport.
 b Melissa looks like her sister.
 c Melissa's sister is lazy.
4 Michael is looking through the photos because …
 a he loves looking at old photos.
 b he wants to show the photos to Melissa.
 c he's doing a project for school.
5 What's different about Michael now?
 a The colour of his hair.
 b The length of his hair.
 c The style of his hair.
6 Michael doesn't like his mum's ___ in the old photo.
 a clothes
 b nose
 c hairstyle

4 ● 1.15 **Listen and number the sentences in the order you hear them.**

 a I'm like him.
 b She's like you.
 c I look like him.
 d I like him.
 e She looks like you.
 f She likes you.

5 ● 1.16 **Listen. Then practise the dialogue.**

Sally Who do you look like in your family?
Phil I look like my brother. We've got the same blond, curly hair and we're both quite tall.
Sally And what about personality? Who do you take after?
Phil I'm more like my mum. We're both quite shy and neither of us is keen on sport. What about you?
Sally I'm more like my dad. We're both very sporty, and we both love travelling. We're also very sociable and we like meeting people.
Phil And who do you look like?
Sally I don't look anything like my mum. I look more like my dad. We're both tall and we've got the same eyes and nose.

6 **ACTIVATE Prepare answers to the questions in blue in exercise 5 using information about you and your family. Then practise your new dialogue with a partner.**

1 Read adverts A–D. For each advert, answer questions 1–3.

1 What type of place is the advert for?

2 What can you do there?

3 What special offer has it got?

A

THE COCONUT CLUB

Dance to the music of the 80s

Free entry if you're wearing 80s clothes!

Mondays and Wednesdays 8 till late

B

THE PICTURE PALACE

Classic and modern horror films

Every night at midnight

Tickets £4 (Usual price £7)

C

PIZZA PRONTO

Buy one pizza, get one free

(Tuesdays and Thursdays only)

5 p.m. – 7 p.m.

D

Silver Boots

Disco on ice

Only £4 (including boot hire)

Free drink with entry before 9 p.m. every day

2 ● 1.29 Listen to a conversation between Hayley and Louise. Which of the places in exercise 1 do they mention?

3 ● 1.29 Study the key phrases. Then listen to the conversation again and write *true* or *false* for 1–6. Correct the false sentences.

> **KEY PHRASES** ○ Changing a plan
>
> Are you still coming?
> What's happening on (Wednesday)?
> I can't make it.
> Something's come up.
> Can we do it another time?
> How about … instead?
> Is … any good for you?

1 Hayley has just been doing some exercise.

2 Louise and Tom have just split up.

3 Louise and Tom went out with each other for over three years.

4 Hayley can't make it on Friday.

5 Hayley and Louise agree to meet on Thursday instead.

6 Louise is going out with Gemma on Friday.

4 ● 1.30 Listen. Then practise the dialogue.

Steph Are you still coming on Wednesday night?

Mark Why? What's happening on Wednesday night?

Steph We're going to The Picture Palace to watch a horror film, remember?

Mark Oh, I'm really sorry, but I can't make it.

Steph But we planned it two weeks ago!

Mark I know, but something's come up. Can we do it another time?

Steph Well, I suppose so.

Mark How about next week instead? Is Friday any good for you?

Steph Yes, that's fine with me.

Mark Great. I'm sorry about Wednesday, Steph.

Steph Oh, don't worry.

5 ACTIVATE **Change the words in blue in exercise 4. Use the places in exercise 1 or your own ideas. Then practise your new dialogue with a partner.**

EXTRA LISTENING AND SPEAKING ● Joining a health club

I can ask for information and give personal details.

③

1 Imagine that you want to join a health club. What information do you need? What questions would you ask the receptionist?

2 ● 2.02 Listen to the conversation. Are any of your questions from exercise 1 mentioned?

3 ● 2.02 Study the key phrases. Then listen to the conversation again. Complete the missing information in the form.

> **KEY PHRASES ○ Joining a health club**
>
> I'm interested in joining the club.
> Could you tell me when you are open?
> How do you spell your first name / surname?
> What's your date of birth?
> Can I take a contact number, please?
> Is ... convenient?

MEMBERSHIP FORM

First name: ¹...

Surname: ²...

Date of birth: ³...

Address: ⁴...

Contact number: ⁵......................................

Mobile number: ⁶.......................................

Email: ⁷...

Time of appointment: ⁸..............................

Personal trainer: ⁹.....................................

Option: ¹⁰...

4 ● 2.03 Listen and write six dates of birth.

5 ● 2.04 Listen. Then practise the dialogue.

Receptionist	Good morning, Active Health Club. How can I help you?
Anne	I'm interested in joining your club. Could you tell me when you are open?
Receptionist	The club is open all day from 10 a.m. to 10 p.m. First you'll need to complete a questionnaire. We can do that over the phone. What's your name?
Anne	Anne Rousseau.
Receptionist	How do you spell your surname, please?
Anne	It's R – O – U – S – S – E – A – U.
Receptionist	What's your date of birth?
Anne	It's the sixth of August, 1993.
Receptionist	Can I take a contact number, please?
Anne	It's 0399 7630921.
Receptionist	Right. I can make an appointment for you now. Have you got an email address?
Anne	Yes, it's anne-rousseau@bmail.com.

6 ACTIVATE Prepare answers to the receptionist's questions in blue in exercise 5 using information about yourself. Then practise your new dialogue with a partner.

EXTRA LISTENING AND SPEAKING ● Buying a coach ticket [4]

I can ask about coach timetables and buy a ticket.

1 Look at the information screen. Which information in the box does it show?

> departure bay   destination   arrival time
> services available on the coach   fares
> departure time   number of stops

	Destination	Bay	Departs	Arrives	Facilities
❶	Newport	5	10.15	13.25	WC
❷	Edinburgh	11	10.25	17.45	WC, TV
❸	Derby	7	10.30	12.55	–
❹	Birmingham	2	10.50	13.05	–
❺	Cardiff	5	11.00	14.30	WC
❻	Derby	7	11.20	13.45	–
❼	Truro	8	11.35	18.50	WC, TV

2 ● 2.17 Listen to two conversations. Answer questions 1 and 2 for each one.

1 Which coach from the screen is the passenger travelling on?
2 Has the passenger got a *Young Person's Coachcard*?

3 ● 2.17 Study the key phrases. Then listen again and choose the correct answers (1–5).

> **KEY PHRASES ○ Buying a coach ticket**
>
> What time does the next coach leave?
> What bay does it leave from?
> A single / return to ... , please.
> When are you coming back?
> What time does it get in?
> Do I have to change?
> No, it's direct.

1 The first passenger wants ...
  a to visit Newport.
  b an earlier coach.
  c a direct coach.
2 The direct coach to Cardiff ...
  a gets to Cardiff later than the Newport coach.
  b gets to Cardiff earlier than the Newport coach.
  c leaves at 14.30.
3 How much does the first passenger's ticket cost?
  a £9.04
  b £19.04
  c £9.40
4 The second passenger wants to come back ...
  a in a month.
  b on the 23rd.
  c in 23 days.
5 The second passenger wants ...
  a a direct coach.
  b the first coach.
  c a later coach.

4 ● 2.18 Listen and write the departure and arrival times you hear.

5 ● 2.19 Listen. Then practise the dialogue.

Passenger What time does the next coach to Ipswich leave?
Assistant Ipswich? Let's see. You can get one at 14.25.
Passenger What time does it get in?
Assistant That coach gets into Ipswich at 16.05.
Passenger Do I have to change?
Assistant No, it's direct. Do you want a single or return?
Passenger A single, please.
Assistant Have you got a *Young Person's Coachcard*?
Passenger No, I haven't.
Assistant OK. That'll be £24.50 then.
Passenger What bay does it leave from?
Assistant Number 5, just by the newspaper stand.

6 ACTIVATE Change the words in blue in exercise 5. Use the information in exercise 1 and decide where you want to travel to. Then practise your new dialogue with a partner.

EXTRA LISTENING AND SPEAKING ● Discussing music

I can understand and talk about tastes in music.

1 Look at the words in the box. Which ones are <u>not</u> types of music?

> pop stone classical hip hop yellows
> rap punk blues heavy metal dirt
> rock jazz

2 ● 2.30 Listen to a conversation between Jake and his dad. What kind of music does Jake like? What kind of music does his dad like?

3 ● 2.30 Study the key phrases. Then listen to the conversation again and choose the correct answers (1–5).

> **KEY PHRASES ○ Talking about music**
>
> I've never heard of them.
> What sort of music is it?
> The lyrics are …
> They write the songs themselves.
> It was released …
> I reckon they're going to be really big.

1 Jake's dad ___ the band.
  a used to listen to   **b** has heard of
  c doesn't know

2 Where did Jake first hear their music?
  a On his computer.   **b** At a gig.
  c On their album.

3 When was their debut album released?
  a A while ago.   **b** Last month.
  c Last week.

4 What does Jake's dad think about the song?
  a It's got no rhythm.   **b** It's too noisy.
  c The lyrics are shocking.

5 What's Jake's opinion of his dad's taste in music?
  a It's boring.   **b** It's exciting.
  c It's relaxing.

4 ● 2.31 Listen and write the adjectives you hear in sentences 1–6.

5 ● 2.32 Listen. Then practise the dialogue.

Guy What are you listening to?

Shona A rapper that I'm really into at the moment – Dizzee Rascal. He's had quite a few number one hits. I love his music.

Guy I've never heard of him. Where's he from?

Shona I think he's from London.

Guy What sort of music is it?

Shona It's a mixture of rap and hip hop. The lyrics are really clever. He writes them himself.

Guy Have you got any of his albums?

Shona Yes, the latest one. It was only released last month. I saw him on TV, then I bought his album.

Guy Have you ever been to one of his gigs?

Shona No, I've never been to a live performance, but I'd like to. He's due to go on tour later this year, so I'll make sure I get tickets.

6 ACTIVATE **Prepare answers to the questions in blue in exercise 5. Use information about your favourite music. Then practise your new dialogue with a partner.**

EXTRA LISTENING AND SPEAKING ● Doing an interview

I can interview an election candidate.

6

1 Match ideas 1–3 with three of the topics in the box.

> health   public transport   education
> environment   jobs

1 lower the price of train tickets
2 build gyms and sports centres
3 raise salaries for young people

2 🔘 3.02 **Listen to an interview with Boris. What is the UKYP? Which ideas in exercise 1 does Boris mention?**

3 🔘 3.02 **Study the key phrases. Then listen to the interview again and choose the correct answers (1–5).**

> **KEY PHRASES ○ Interviewing an election candidate**
>
> Can I ask you some questions about …
> What do you feel strongly about?
> I see. In that case, …
> What changes would you make?
> How would that improve things?
> I see what you mean, but …
> My final question is this: …

1 Boris says that he ___ interested in politics.
  a 's only   b isn't really
  c isn't only
2 The UKYP wants to improve life for …
  a everyone in the UK.
  b all people in Europe.
  c all young British people.
3 Boris says that young people don't use the buses and trains because …
  a they're too expensive.
  b of the effect on the environment.
  c their parents drive them everywhere.
4 Boris thinks there should be more buses in …
  a the countryside.   b cities.
  c both the countryside and cities.
5 Boris thinks he'll be a good candidate because he's …
  a optimistic.   b reliable.
  c successful.

4 🔘 3.03 **Listen and write the letters you hear. Do you know what the abbreviations stand for?**

5 🔘 3.04 **Listen. Then practise the dialogue.**

Interviewer Can I ask you some questions about your policies? What do you feel strongly about?

Caitlin Education, because young people won't be successful unless they get a good education.

Interviewer I see. In that case, what changes would you make?

Caitlin I'd spend more money on IT in schools and I'd make sure there's a computer for every student.

Interviewer How would that improve things?

Caitlin Students would get the latest information from the internet and wouldn't use books.

Interviewer My final question is this: what makes you a good election candidate?

Caitlin I get on well with different types of people and I'm good at communicating.

6 **ACTIVATE** Imagine that you're an election candidate. Prepare answers to the questions in blue in exercise 5 using the topics in exercise 1 or your own ideas. Then practise your new interview with a partner.

EXTRA LISTENING AND SPEAKING ● Telling an interesting story

I can understand and tell a story.

1 Complete the email with *who, which, where* or *whose.*

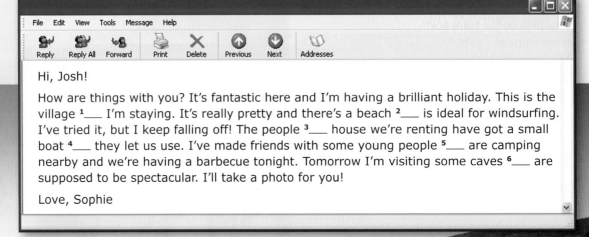

File Edit View Tools Message Help

Reply | Reply All | Forward | Print | Delete | Previous | Next | Addresses

Hi, Josh!

How are things with you? It's fantastic here and I'm having a brilliant holiday. This is the village ¹___ I'm staying. It's really pretty and there's a beach ²___ is ideal for windsurfing. I've tried it, but I keep falling off! The people ³___ house we're renting have got a small boat ⁴___ they let us use. I've made friends with some young people ⁵___ are camping nearby and we're having a barbecue tonight. Tomorrow I'm visiting some caves ⁶___ are supposed to be spectacular. I'll take a photo for you!

Love, Sophie

2 🔘 3.15 Listen to a conversation between Natalie and Lee. Where has Natalie been? Where's Lee going?

3 🔘 3.15 Study the key phrases. Then listen to the conversation again and answer the questions (1–6).

> **KEY PHRASES ○ Telling a story**
>
> That reminds me.
> You'll never guess what happened.
> Guess who ...
> No way!
> Honestly! It was him / her.
> You mean to say you actually ... ?

1 What was the weather like in the UK while Natalie was away?
2 What sports did she do on holiday?
3 Where did Natalie see Rafael Nadal?
4 What was he like?
5 What language did Natalie and Rafael speak? Why?
6 Which places did he talk about?

4 🔘 3.16 Listen. Then practise the dialogue.

Lydia You'll never guess what happened to me the other day while I was going to London.
Mike What?
Lydia Well, I was on the train and I was buying something to eat. Anyway, guess who stood next to me.
Mike I've got no idea.
Lydia Alesha Dixon, the pop star!
Mike No way!
Lydia Honestly! It was her. She was really friendly and interesting.
Mike You mean to say you actually spoke to her?
Lydia Yes, we chatted a bit about her music.
Mike Then what happened?
Lydia She said, 'Have a good time in London.'

5 ACTIVATE **Change the words in blue in exercise 4 using your own ideas. Then practise your new dialogue with a partner.**

EXTRA LISTENING AND SPEAKING ■ Dealing with money

I can pay for things and check the change.

8

1 Look at the price lists A–C. Where do you think they are from?

2 🔘 3.28 Read problems 1–3. Then listen to two dialogues. For each dialogue say what the problem is, and which price list from exercise 1 is mentioned.

1 The assistant calculates the total wrongly.
2 The customer hasn't got enough money.
3 The assistant gives too much change.

3 🔘 3.28 Study the key phrases. Then listen again and answer the questions (1–5).

> **KEY PHRASES ◯ Paying for things**
>
> I make that …
> I'm terribly sorry.
> Not to worry.
> I owe you …
> I think you've given me too much change.

1 What does the first customer order?
2 Where is the first customer going to sit?
3 What does she say when the assistant apologizes?
4 What couldn't the second customer see?
5 What excuse does the second assistant make?

A

Magazines & Newspapers
                    See individual prices
Stamps   31p, 39p
Phonecard (UK & International)
                £5, £10, £20
Envelopes   £1.20 per packet

B

oranges   6 for €1.50
apples   8 for €1.49
melon   €1.49 each
pineapple €1.80 each

C

	small	large
Hot chocolate	£1.75	£2.50
Coffee	£1.50	£2.25
Tea	£1.40	£1.90
Apple juice	80p	£1.50
Muffins, cookies	£1.00 each	
Sandwiches	£2.50 each	

4 🔘 3.29 Listen to the sentences and write the prices you hear.

5 🔘 3.30 Listen. Then practise the dialogue. What mistake has the assistant made?

Customer   A melon and three oranges, please.
Assistant   Anything else?
Customer   No, that's everything, thanks.
Assistant   OK, that's €2.44, please.
Customer   Here you are.
Assistant   And 56 cents change.
Customer   Excuse me, I think you've overcharged me.
Assistant   Let's see. €1.49 for the melon, and 75 cents for the oranges.
Customer   I make that €2.24.
Assistant   Oh yes, you're quite right. So I owe you 20 cents. I'm terribly sorry.
Customer   Not to worry.

6 ACTIVATE Change the words in blue in exercise 5 using the information in exercise 1 or your own ideas. Then practise your new dialogue with a partner.

CURRICULUM EXTRA ● History: The Berlin Wall
I can understand people talking about their personal experiences of the Berlin Wall.

A DIVIDED CITY

In 1949, after the Second World War, Germany was divided into two countries: West Germany and East Germany. Berlin was the largest city and it was also divided into West Berlin and East Berlin. The ¹___ was higher in West Germany and West Berlin, so many people who were living in East Germany chose to move. By 1961, around 20% of the population of East Germany had left for a better life, either in West Germany or West Berlin.

The East German Government wanted to stop so many people leaving the country. They had already closed the main ²___ with West Germany, but on 13th August 1961, they installed a temporary ³___ between West Berlin and East Berlin. Days later, the East German army built a permanent ⁴___ wall there – the Berlin Wall. People who were living in East Berlin weren't allowed to travel to the West, or to have any contact with people living there.

For twenty-eight years, people living in the East and West had completely separate lives. Life in East Germany was hard. There were food ⁵___ and the secret police monitored people's lives. During this time, around 5,000 people escaped from East to West Berlin. However, ⁶___ killed around 100 people as they were trying to get over the wall.

By 1989, other countries had begun to open their borders between Eastern and Western Europe. On 9th November 1989, the East German Government allowed people to cross the wall into West Berlin. Thousands of people heard the news and came to the wall, where they met friends and family who they hadn't seen for years. Many people started to pull down the wall in a celebration of the ⁷___ of their city.

1 Check the meaning of the words in the box. Then complete the text.

> barbed wire fence border reunification
> guards standard of living concrete
> shortages

2 🔘 1.17 Read and listen to the text. Check your answers to exercise 1.

3 Read the text again and answer the questions.

   1 How was Berlin similar to Germany in 1949?

   2 Why did many people in East Germany want to move to the West?

   3 What did the East German Government do in 1961 to stop people leaving?

   4 Why did people in East Germany have less privacy than people in the West?

   5 How many people escaped from East to West Berlin?

   6 When did the Berlin Wall open?

   7 What did some people do when it opened?

4 🔘 1.18 Listen to two people talking about their experiences. Who used to live in East Berlin? Listen again and complete the sentences with L (Liesel) or H (Hans).

   1 ___ lived in West Berlin.

   2 ___ used to have a job in West Berlin.

   3 ___ had relatives on the other side of the wall.

   4 ___ wanted to move.

   5 ___ has got a piece of the Berlin Wall.

   6 ___ knew someone who escaped over the wall.

   7 ___ never crossed the border until the wall opened.

5 ACTIVATE Imagine that your town, city or country is divided by a wall. Complete the sentences with your own ideas.

   1 When I saw them building the wall, I felt ___.

   2 I tried to ___, but ___.

   3 Before they built the wall, people used to ___.

   4 My family was affected because ___.

   5 Things are different now because ___.

CURRICULUM EXTRA ● Language and literature: The realist novel

I can understand an extract from a novel.

1 Look at the photo from a film adaptation of an English novel. In which period of history do you think the novel is set? Why? Then read the paragraph below and check.

Realist novels describe fictional people and events in real places during particular periods of history. They give the reader a realistic picture of society at that time. *Pride and Prejudice* is a realist novel set in the south of England in the early 19th century. It describes the relationships of the Bennet sisters. Its author, Jane Austen, was one of the most famous English realist novelists.

2 🔘 1.31 Read and listen to the text. What is Mrs Bennet's news?

3 Read the text again and write *true* or *false*. Correct the false sentences.

1 Families with unmarried daughters consider men with a lot of money as good future husbands.
2 Mr Bennet doesn't know who is moving in to Netherfield Park.
3 The Bennets' house is finer than Netherfield Park.
4 Bingley and his servants are arriving on Monday.
5 Mrs Bennet is pleased that the young man is going to live in Netherfield Park.
6 All the Bennet girls are married.

4 **ACTIVATE** Think about a famous novelist from your country. Answer questions 1–4.

1 What are his / her most famous novels?
2 What period of history are his / her novels set in?
3 What sort of people did he / she write about?
4 What sort of things happen in his / her novels?

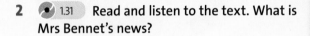

Pride and Prejudice by Jane Austen

It is a truth well known to all the world that an unmarried man in possession of a large fortune must be in need of a wife. And when such a man comes to a neighbourhood, even if nothing is known about his feelings or opinions, this truth is so clear to the surrounding families, that they think of him immediately as the future husband of one of their daughters.

'My dear Mr Bennet,' said Mrs Bennet to her husband one day. 'Have you heard that someone is going to rent Netherfield Park at last?'

'No, Mrs Bennet, I haven't,' said her husband.

'Don't you want to know who is renting it?' cried Mrs Bennet impatiently.

'You want to tell me, and I don't mind listening.' Mrs Bennet needed no more encouragement. 'Well, my dear, I hear that he's a very rich young man from the north of England. It seems he came to see Netherfield on Monday and was so delighted with it that he arranged to rent it immediately. Of course, it is the finest house in the area with the largest gardens. His servants will be here by the end of the week, and he will be arriving soon afterwards!'

'What is his name?' asked Mr Bennet.

'Bingley.'

'Is he married or single?'

'Oh, single my dear, of course. A single man of large fortune – he has an income of four or five thousand pounds a year. How wonderful for our girls!'

'Why? How can it affect them?' Mr Bennet asked.

'My dear Mr Bennet, how can you be so annoying? You must realize that I'm thinking of his marrying one of our daughters!'

CURRICULUM EXTRA ● Biology: Healthy eating
I can talk about healthy eating.

3

1 **Match definitions 1–5 with the words in** blue **in the text.**

1 Made from milk.
2 Made in a factory.
3 Groups of cells of particular types.
4 Information which proves something.
5 The part of food we don't digest.

2 ● 2.05 **Read and listen to the text. How does healthy eating affect our lives?**

3 **Read the text again and choose the correct answers.**

1 A healthy diet can …
  a help to prevent heart disease.
  b increase the risk of depression.
  c reduce the need for exercise.
2 What type of food is the main source of vitamins?
  a Oily fish.
  b Carbohydrates.
  c Fruit and vegetables.
3 We need around ___ of our daily diet to be protein.
  a one third
  b 15%
  c five portions
4 Why do we need oily fish or nuts in our diet?
  a To provide calories.
  b To absorb vitamins.
  c To increase cholesterol levels.
5 Which fats are not good for us?
  a Saturated fats.
  b Unsaturated fats.
  c Omega-3 fatty acids.
6 What has the most influence on the way we feel?
  a The type of food we eat.
  b Eating regular meals.
  c Eating breakfast every day.

4 **ACTIVATE Complete the sentences about your diet. Discuss how healthy or unhealthy your diet is. What should you change?**

1 I eat a lot of ___ and ___.
2 I never eat ___ or ___.
3 My favourite foods are ___ and ___.
4 I have at least ___ snacks a day.
5 I ___ eat regular meals.

Have you got the balance right?

Healthy eating really does keep the doctor away and it may also help us feel better. A balanced diet along with regular exercise can reduce the risk of illnesses such as heart disease, diabetes and perhaps even depression. The human body needs three essential types of nutrient – protein, fat and carbohydrates – as well as fibre, vitamins and minerals. The key to healthy eating is getting the balance right between the different types of food. The perfect balance is to eat plenty of fruit, vegetables and carbohydrates, some dairy foods, meat and fish, but to go easy on the fats and sugars.

Nutritionists say we should eat at least five portions of fruit and vegetables a day to get all the vitamins and minerals we need. These also provide fibre which helps us digest our food and control our weight. Carbohydrates, such as bread, pasta and potatoes, provide calories and other nutrients and should make up at least a third of our diet. While protein is essential for building and repairing tissues, it only needs to make up about 15% of an adult diet. The body needs fat to absorb some vitamins, and some fats like omega-3 fatty acids are essential for the brain and may even help learning. Foods rich in unsaturated fats, such as oily fish and nuts, are better than saturated animal fats which increase harmful cholesterol levels in our blood. Processed foods are particularly unhealthy because they are full of fats, sugar and salt and are very high in calories.

So far, there is little evidence to show that the type of food we eat affects our mood. But studies show that eating three meals a day affects the way we feel. Scientists believe that eating breakfast regularly is even more important. Studies show that it improves our mood and memory, gives us more energy and helps us to feel more relaxed. So if you want to feel good throughout the day, don't miss your breakfast!

CURRICULUM EXTRA ● Physics and chemistry: Satellites and spacecraft

4

I can talk about the future of space travel and exploration.

1 Check the meaning of the words in the box. Then match them with A–E in the photos.

> space station   weightlessness
> space shuttle   Earth   satellite

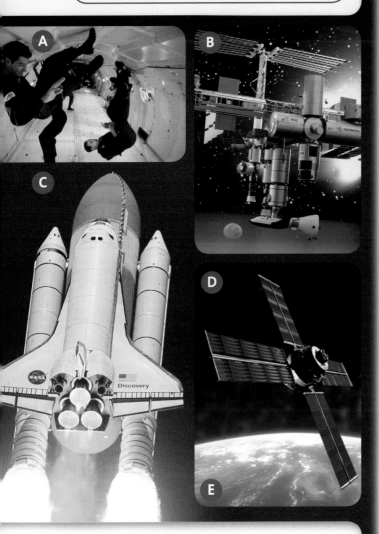

Out of this world

A **¹**___ is an object that orbits another object in space. There are natural satellites like the moon, which orbits **²**___, and there are also artificial satellites. Artificial satellites are man-made objects which are sent into space. In 1957, the Soviet Union launched the first artificial satellite, *Sputnik 1*, and today there are about three thousand artificial satellites in orbit around Earth. We use them to transmit phone calls and TV signals across the world, to navigate journeys, to forecast the weather, and to study the universe.

The largest artificial satellite in orbit is the International **³**___ or ISS. The American **⁴**___ started taking material into space to build the ISS there in the late 1990s, and different teams of researchers have lived there continuously since November 2000. The ISS was also the destination of the world's first space tourists. One of them, the Hungarian-American billionaire Charles Simonyi, enjoyed the visit so much that he paid $35 million for a second trip. During his visits to space, he helped with research projects and chatted to schoolchildren in the USA via a video link.

Space tourism will be more popular in the future, thanks to the development of sub-orbital spacecraft. Travelling to altitudes of over one hundred kilometres, these craft reach the boundaries of space, at the edge of the Earth's atmosphere. From there, passengers get a breathtaking view of Earth, and can also experience **⁵**___. Prices started at $200,000 for a three-hour trip, but flights will certainly become cheaper in the future. Scientists hope that the increase in space tourism will help to raise money to fund further space projects.

2 ● 2.20 **Complete the text with the words in exercise 1. Then read and listen to the text and check.**

3 Read the text again and write *true* or *false*. Correct the false sentences.

1 The Soviet Union put the first artificial satellite in orbit.
2 *Sputnik 1* was the first natural satellite.
3 Astronauts constructed the ISS in space.
4 Teams of researchers have been living in space since 1990.
5 Charles Simonyi has been on one trip into space.
6 Sub-orbital spacecraft are spaceships which travel into space.
7 People can experience weightlessness on sub-orbital spacecraft.

4 ACTIVATE Read sentences 1–6. Work in pairs and discuss whether you think these things are already possible, will be possible in the future, or will never be possible.

1 Hotels will open in space.
2 Tourists will be able to visit other planets.
3 People will have their own personal space shuttle.
4 People will be able to experience weightlessness in their own home.
5 People will grow plants in space.
6 There will be budget flights to the moon costing about €100.

CURRICULUM EXTRA ● History: Child labour
I can talk about child labour laws in my country.

A hard life

The Industrial Revolution started in Britain in the 18th century. This was the social and economic transformation of the nation from an agricultural to an industrial society. The production of textiles became very important and many huge cotton mills were built. Thousands of workers were employed in them, including a large number of children. Child labour wasn't a new phenomenon; children from working-class families had always worked to earn money as soon as they were old enough. They were usually employed locally in houses and shops, or on farms.

However, working life in the cotton mills was often much worse for children than before. They usually lived away from their families, and children as young as five were employed. They were small enough to get under the huge machines and pick up loose pieces of cotton. This was a very dangerous job, and many children were killed or injured by the machinery. Children often worked up to twenty hours a day in the mills. If they sat down or fell asleep, they were punished and their low wages were reduced or stopped. Orphans and homeless children weren't paid at all – food and a bed were considered enough for them.

These conditions may seem appalling to us today, but most of the mill owners didn't think about the children they were exploiting. There were no laws to protect children in the workplace, so they weren't breaking the law. In many countries today, there are strict laws on how old children have to be to work, and how many hours a week they can work. However, child labour in the textile industry isn't completely a thing of the past. In some countries, young children continue to work long hours in clothes factories to meet the demand for cheap clothing.

1 Check the meaning of the words in bold. Then choose the correct answers.

During the Industrial Revolution in Britain, a lot of [1]**working-class** / **upper-class** children worked in [2]**machinery** / **cotton mills**. [3]**Orphans** / **Mill owners** didn't usually receive any [4]**wages** / **factories** and there weren't any laws about [5]**textiles** / **child labour**.

2 🔘 2.33 Read and listen to the text. Check your answers to exercise 1.

3 Read the text again and answer the questions.

1 Why were cotton mills built in Britain?
2 Where did working-class children usually work before the Industrial Revolution?
3 Why did mill owners employ very young children?
4 What happened to children if they stopped working?
5 What did the orphans receive instead of wages?
6 Were the mill owners doing anything illegal? Explain your answer.
7 Has child labour stopped now? Explain your answer.

4 ACTIVATE Read the laws about child labour in the UK. Do you think the rules are a good idea or not? Explain your answers. What are the rules in your country?

1 You must be over fourteen years old to work.

2 You mustn't work before seven o'clock in the morning or after seven o'clock at night.

3 You mustn't work in a factory, a mine or a ship.

4 You mustn't work during school hours on a school day.

5 You mustn't work for more than two hours on a school day or a Sunday.

6 You mustn't work for more than four hours a day without a break of one hour.

English Plus Options

CURRICULUM EXTRA ◼ Language and literature: Word building: adjectives **6**
I can form adjectives using suffixes.

1 **Check the meaning of the words in the box. Then complete the text.**

> proudly   army   dishonesty   neighbours
> customs   murder   judges   laws

2 🔘 3.05 **Read and listen to the text. Check your answers to exercise 1.**

3 **Read the text again and write *true* or *false*. Correct the false sentences.**
1 The King of Brobdingnag is interested in Gulliver's country.
2 The head of state in Gulliver's country is a king.
3 Gulliver's country has no agriculture.
4 Gulliver describes the political and legal systems in his country.
5 Gulliver's country is rarely at war.
6 The King of Brobdingnag admires Gulliver's country.

4 **Complete the table with adjectives from the text. Then write the adjective suffixes.**

Related word	Adjective	Suffix
interest	interesting	-ing
intelligence	1 ___	2 ___
understand	3 ___	4 ___
politics	5 ___	6 ___
delight	7 ___	8 ___
enjoy	9 ___	10 ___
peace	11 ___	12 ___

5 **ACTIVATE Complete the sentences with an adjective. Use suffixes from exercise 4. Which suffixes do you use to form adjectives in your language? Give examples.**
1 *Gulliver's Travels* is an ___ work of fiction. (interest)
2 The country was ruled by a ___ king. (power)
3 The King ruled three countries, but they were small and ___. (manage)
4 The King is very ___ in the customs of Gulliver's country. (interest)
5 He explained the ___ customs of his country to the King. (tradition)

Gulliver's Travels *Jonathan Swift*

Gulliver reaches Brobdingnag, a land of giants.

In the next few weeks, I began to have some very interesting conversations with the King. He was an intelligent, understanding person.

'Tell me more about your country,' he said to me one day. 'I would like to hear about your laws, your political life, and your ¹___ and traditions. Tell me everything. There may be something that we can usefully copy here in Brobdingnag.'

'I shall be delighted, sir,' I answered ²___. 'Our king controls our three great countries, Scotland, Ireland and England. We grow much of our own food, and our weather is neither too hot nor too cold. There are two groups of men who make our ³___. One is called the House of Lords – they are men from the oldest and greatest families in the country. The other is called the House of Commons – these are the most honest, intelligent, and sensible men in the country, and are freely chosen by the people. We have ⁴___ to decide punishments for criminals, and we have a large ⁵___, which cannot be defeated by any other in the world.'

While I was talking, the King was making notes. For several days I continued my explanation, and I also described British history over the last hundred years. Then the King asked me a large number of questions.

'Why,' he asked, 'are you so often at war? Either you find fighting enjoyable, or you have very difficult ⁶___! Why do you need an army at all? You would not be afraid of any other country if you were peaceful people. And in the last hundred years, you've done nothing but rob, fight and ⁷___! Your recent history shows the very worst effects of cruelty, jealousy, ⁸___ and madness!'

English **Plus** Options

CURRICULUM EXTRA ● Biology: The brain
I can understand a text about the brain and its functions.

7

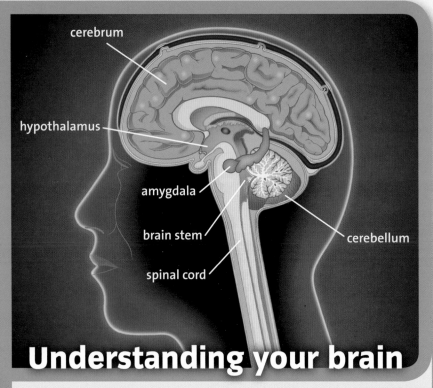

cerebrum

hypothalamus

amygdala

brain stem

cerebellum

spinal cord

Understanding your brain

Every animal has a brain, but the human brain is unique. It controls everything we do, think or feel and allows us to speak and imagine. It constantly analyses and responds to messages from outside and inside the body.

The three main parts of the brain – the brain stem, the cerebellum and the cerebrum – have evolved over millions of years. The brain stem is the most primitive part that we share with all animals. It links the rest of the brain to the spinal cord and controls involuntary body functions like breathing and digestion, as well as basic instincts like danger. It may be responsible for phobias, which scientists think are primitive survival instincts.

Next to evolve was the cerebellum at the back of the brain. It isn't very large, but it contains over half of all the brain cells, or neurones, and deals with huge amounts of information. It controls balance, movement and coordination and without it we couldn't stand or walk straight.

The largest and final part of the brain to develop was the cerebrum. This is the centre of thinking, memory and language, and it is highly specialized in humans. It is this part that makes us more intelligent than other animals. The cerebrum is divided into two hemispheres which each control opposite sides of the body and seem to have slightly different functions. The right hemisphere helps us think about creative things like music, art and shapes, while the left side is better at maths, logic and language.

Other smaller parts of the brain also have important functions. The hypothalamus is essential for keeping our body temperature constant, while the amygdala below it controls our emotions.

The human brain is incredibly complex and scientists are only just starting to understand it. A lot more research is needed to complete the picture.

1 Match definitions 1–5 with the words in blue in the text.

1 Always the same.
2 Extremely old and not highly developed.
3 Not consciously controlled.
4 Halves.
5 Developed and changed gradually over time.

2 ⏺ 3.17 Read and listen to the text. What are the three main parts of the brain called?

3 Read the text again and answer the questions.

1 Which part of the body does the brain stem connect to the rest of the brain?
2 What body functions does the brain stem control?
3 Where are the majority of the brain's neurones?
4 Which part of the brain was the last to develop?
5 Why does the cerebrum make humans unique?
6 What would happen if the hypothalamus was damaged?

4 **ACTIVATE** Work with a partner and decide which parts of the brain are responsible for 1–6.

1 A fear of snakes.
2 Being good at drawing.
3 Being good at solving problems.
4 Being able to ride a bike.
5 Feeling unhappy.
6 Keeping cool in hot weather.

CURRICULUM EXTRA ● Civic and ethical education: Moral values

I can talk and write about a moral dilemma.

8

1 Check the meaning of the words in the box. Then complete the text.

> deceived trust envious
> consequences reward
> identities unfair

2 🔘 3.31 Read and listen to the text. Check your answers to exercise 1.

3 Read the text again and write M (Marc), J (Jasmine), P (their parents) or N (no one) for sentences 1–7.

1 ___ didn't get good exam results.
2 ___ acted dishonestly.
3 ___ experienced negative emotions about what had happened.
4 ___ didn't find out that Jasmine had cheated.
5 ___ had a difficult decision.
6 ___ broke a promise.
7 ___ benefited from someone else's moral values.

4 Work with a partner and discuss questions 1–6.

1 If you were Marc, what would you have done? Why?
2 Does it make a difference that Jasmine is Marc's sister?
3 What would you do if you were Jasmine's mum or dad and you found out what had happened?
4 Can you think of a reason why Jasmine cheated?
5 Is it important to keep a promise? Why / Why not?
6 Have you ever been in a situation like this? What happened?

5 **ACTIVATE** Write about a moral dilemma that you have experienced. Describe the situation and what you did. What happened in the end?

A moral dilemma

Life is full of decisions, but some are more difficult than others. Sometimes we have to make a decision where every option seems like a bad one, and those are the most difficult of all.

Marc and his sister Jasmine had important exams at school recently. Marc studied hard, but he found the exams difficult and his results were poor. However, Jasmine's results were much better. Her parents were delighted and bought her a new computer as a ¹___. Marc was a bit ²___ – he'd worked hard too – but he was pleased for his sister. However, a few weeks later, Jasmine admitted to Marc that she had cheated in the exams. She made him promise not to say anything. Marc was shocked and angry that Jasmine had ³___ everyone, particularly their parents. However, he knew that Jasmine would hate him if he broke his promise. In the end, although he felt that it was completely ⁴___, he decided to keep quiet.

In situations like this, the action that a person takes will depend on their moral values. These are the principles that make us decide what are the right and wrong things to do. In the same way that people have different appearances and personalities, we have different moral ⁵___. A value that is extremely important to one person, such as honesty, might not be as important to another person. In Marc's situation, he faced a moral dilemma, but his moral values helped him to make a decision. He strongly wanted Jasmine to face the ⁶___ of her actions, but he felt that breaking his sister's ⁷___ would be even worse. Jasmine was lucky – other people might feel that uncovering her dishonesty was the most important thing.

CULTURE ■ Britain in the 1960s
I can plan and give a presentation about the Noughties.

1   Look at photos A and B and answer the questions.

A

1   Who are these people?
2   Who or what do you think they are looking at?

B

1   What do you think this person's job is?
2   Why do you think people chose her for the job?

2   ⏺ 1.19   Read and listen to the text. Check your answers to exercise 1.

The Swinging Sixties

Life in Britain after the Second World War wasn't easy. During the 1940s, food was rationed, which meant that people could only buy small amounts of food such as butter, meat and sugar. Clothes were also rationed until 1949 because there wasn't enough material to produce new ones. However, at the start of the 1960s things started to change. Rationing had ended in 1954 and by the end of the decade the economy was recovering. There were plenty of jobs and more goods in the shops than ever before. There was a general mood of hope and optimism in the country and this increased when England won the football World Cup for the first time in 1966. Britain had become a vibrant and exciting place and the centre of a provocative new youth culture. The new fashions symbolized these changes. Clothes became more brightly coloured and fun, and the miniskirt and the bikini arrived on the scene. Trendy new boutiques opened on London's King's Road and Carnaby Street. They sold very fashionable clothes to a new generation of stylish young people. This was also the era of Lesley Hornby, who became the fashion icon of the 60s with her boyish looks. Her childhood nickname was 'Twiggy' because she was so thin and she became the world's first supermodel at the age of sixteen.

There was also a revolution in British music in the 1960s. American rock and roll had dominated the music scene in the 1950s, but suddenly The Beatles, a band from Liverpool, became the latest craze. Wherever they went there was hysteria, which people called 'Beatlemania'. People screamed so loudly at their concerts that they could hardly hear the music! Beatlemania reached the USA, too. When The Beatles sang live on TV there in 1964, around 74 million viewers watched – that was about half of the population. The 1960s became known in Britain as 'the swinging sixties' – a time when the country was at the centre of the world for fashion, pop music and culture.

3   Read the text again and answer the questions.

1   What did rationing mean for people?
2   How many times had England won the football World Cup before 1966?
3   How did fashion change in the 1960s?
4   Which parts of London were famous for clothes shops?
5   What was Twiggy famous for?
6   What did some people do at The Beatles concerts?
7   Did people in the USA like The Beatles? How do you know?

4   YOUR CULTURE   Answer the questions.

1   Which people in your country were famous in the 1960s?
2   Has the football World Cup ever taken place in your country? When?
3   What fashions were popular in your country in the 1960s?
4   What music was popular in your country in the 1960s?
5   Are The Beatles popular in your country?

5   TASK   Give a presentation about the Noughties.

1   Work in groups of three or four and list a few important events which took place during the Noughties.
2   Make notes about the following things:
    • popular music: types of music, bands, singers
    • fashion trends
    • new technology
    • TV programmes
    • famous people
    • political and social changes.
3   Give your presentation to the rest of the class.
4   Vote for the best presentation.

CULTURE ● Getting married in the UK

I can design a brochure for a wedding venue.

1 Check the meaning of the words in the box. Which things can you see in the photo?

> bride groom church wedding ring
> wedding dress bouquet guests vicar

2 🔘 1.32 Read and listen to the text. What do these numbers refer to?

> 1972 500,000 fourth 14th
> a hundred two thirds

3 Read the text again and answer the questions.

1 Is the number of weddings which take place in the UK each year changing? If so, how?
2 What do people believe will happen to the woman who catches a bride's bouquet?
3 Why do brides often wear something blue?
4 What role does the best man have at a wedding?
5 What do bridesmaids do at a wedding?
6 Where do most civil ceremonies take place?
7 Where can you get married in the UK?

4 YOUR CULTURE Answer the questions.

1 Is marriage as popular as ever in your country? Why / Why not?
2 What traditions are associated with weddings in your country?
3 Which are more popular in your country, civil weddings or religious weddings?
4 Are there any unusual places in your country where people get married?
5 Do you want to get married when you're older? Why / Why not?

5 TASK Design a brochure for an unusual wedding venue.

1 Work in groups and choose a venue.
2 What special services and facilities are there? Include details of costs.
3 Write a short introduction presenting the venue. Say why it is a unique place for a wedding.
4 Choose photos to illustrate your brochure.
5 Present your brochure to the class. Vote for the most popular wedding venue.

Wedding bells

The popularity of marriage in the UK has been declining over recent years. Almost 500,000 couples got married in 1972, but in 2007, there were only 270,000 weddings. It seems that these days more people prefer to live together without getting married.

Today's wedding ceremony dates back to the early 19th century, but many of the traditions associated with weddings are much older. Since the 1100s, the groom has placed the wedding ring on the fourth finger of the bride's left hand. Since the 14th century, the bride has thrown her bouquet towards the female guests. According to superstition, the one who catches it will be the next bride. Also, for more than a hundred years, the bride has worn 'something old, something new, something borrowed and something blue' for good luck.

As well as the bride and groom, other people are important at a wedding. The groom has a 'best man' – usually the groom's brother or a close friend. He's responsible for getting the groom to the wedding on time, and he looks after the rings before the ceremony. The bride often has bridesmaids – friends or relatives who help her to get ready. They walk behind her down the aisle and hold her bouquet during the ceremony. The bride's father is also very important. He makes a speech at the reception after the ceremony and traditionally he pays for everything, although these days many couples pay for their own wedding.

Fewer couples get married in church today and about two thirds of British couples choose a civil ceremony in a government register office. However, it's possible to get married in any public place with a special licence and some places are more unusual than others. Manchester United fans can get married at Old Trafford stadium and animal lovers can do it at London Zoo. You can even get married at Alton Towers, one of the UK's biggest theme parks!

CULTURE ■ Snack culture in the UK
I can make a survey about snacking habits.

1 Match definitions 1–6 with the words in blue in the text.

1 Salty.
2 Something which is difficult to give up.
3 To be responsible.
4 Foods which are quick and easy to prepare.
5 Slow process of damage.
6 Sweet snacks.

2 ● 2.06 Read and listen to the text. Answer the questions.

1 When and where do people in Britain eat snacks?
2 How much is the confectionery market worth in the UK?
3 Why do we like eating snacks?
4 How do manufacturers make their products attractive to consumers?
5 What effect is snacking having on British children?
6 How does eating snacks help to cause obesity?
7 When should we eat snacks?

3 YOUR CULTURE Answer the questions.

1 What snacks are popular in your country?
2 Do most people in your country eat regular meals?
3 When and where do people eat snacks?
4 Where do you buy snacks?
5 Can you buy snacks at school?

4 TASK Make a survey of snacking habits in your class.

1 Work in pairs and prepare a short questionnaire. Write notes about the following and your own ideas:
• favourite snacks
• when and where
• how often
• how much.
2 Interview the other students in your class and make notes of their answers.
3 Write a short summary of the results, or present your information in a graph.

Snacks and convenience foods have become a major part of the UK daily diet. People in Britain no longer eat at a table or at set meal times; they eat on the move while they're doing other things. Kids consume sweets, crisps and fizzy drinks on the way to and from school. Office workers eat a sandwich at their desks. On public transport, in the street, everywhere you go, people are snacking.

The average Briton eats 7.2 kg of snacks each year. Italians, by comparison, eat just 1 kg and Russians even less. The UK savoury snack market alone is worth a massive £2.4 billion a year, with around 27 million packets of crisps, nuts and other snacks eaten every day. Another £6.1 billion is spent on confectionery each year. Bad food is available everywhere, even in places that are not normally associated with food, like chemists and schools, while healthier alternatives are more difficult to find.

Our bodies are genetically programmed to enjoy the tastes of fat, salt and sugar and the food manufacturers make sure that our snacks – chocolate bars, crisps, peanuts, sandwiches, burgers – are full of them. Research suggests that junk food may even be addictive and that some people simply cannot stop eating it.

This snack culture is having disastrous effects on British people's health. Obesity has grown by 300% over the past 20 years and, although rising obesity is a worldwide problem, in the UK the rate is rising faster than almost anywhere else. A third of the total number of obese children in Europe is British and experts say that our eating habits are to blame.

Clearly, eating lots of junk food is not good for us, but now some nutritionists say that the very principle of snacking all day, whether it's healthy or junk food, is the real problem. They say that snacking makes us even hungrier because it interferes with the body's ability to burn fat, therefore causing obesity as well as tooth decay. So what is the answer? It seems that we should go back to having three proper meals a day, with no snacks in between. That's something to remember the next time you fancy a bar of chocolate.

A Nation of Snackers

CULTURE ● Volunteer holidays

I can plan and present a volunteer holiday for a family.

1 Look at the photos. Where are the people and what are they doing?

2 ◉ 2.21 Read and listen to the text. What is voluntourism? Why is it becoming popular?

3 Read the text again and answer the questions.

1 Who used to do volunteer work abroad?
2 How have volunteer projects changed these days?
3 What can child volunteers do?
4 Why is voluntourism good for young people?
5 How do volunteers hope to help communities?
6 Why do some people criticize voluntourism?

4 YOUR CULTURE Answer the questions.

1 Is volunteer work popular in your country?
2 What sort of things do volunteers do?
3 Do you know anyone who has been on a volunteer holiday?
4 Would you like to go on a volunteer holiday? Why / Why not?
5 What kind of holidays do people in your country go on?

5 TASK Plan a volunteer holiday for a family.

1 Work in pairs and plan a volunteer holiday suitable for a family. Choose a suitable destination and type of volunteer work.
2 Write notes about the following features of the holiday and your own ideas:
   • what adults / children can do
   • positive impact of the work
   • accommodation and other facilities
   • length of stay, transport
   • cost of the holiday.
3 Present your volunteer holiday to the rest of the class. Which is the most popular holiday?

Volunteer family holidays

A new type of adventure travel is becoming popular with people who want a different kind of holiday. Volunteer tourism or 'voluntourism' involves doing volunteer work while you are on holiday. In the past, volunteer projects lasted several weeks or months and were mainly for students or skilled people like nurses. Nowadays, however, there are plenty of short-term volunteer holidays for just about every interest or age group, including family-friendly holidays. Instead of swimming in the hotel pool or sunbathing on the beach, you can go to South Africa and study rhinos, work in an elephant sanctuary in Thailand, or help on a construction project in Latin America. Even children can take part by doing simple tasks like cleaning beaches, planting trees or simply spending time working with local children.

A volunteer holiday can be a very rewarding experience for a family. Volunteering as a family is a good way for young people to learn important values like kindness, responsibility and cooperation. By meeting people from around the world and experiencing different cultures, they learn to put their own problems into perspective, especially if they are used to an easy consumer lifestyle. They learn that annoying things in their daily lives, like housework or homework, are nothing compared to the problems that people from poorer countries face every day.

However, not everyone is happy with voluntourism. Some people feel that it may do more harm than good. Voluntourists believe that they make a positive difference by bringing money to local communities and by helping with development projects, but critics argue that voluntourists lack the skills and the time to really understand the problems and make a difference. In some cases they may even replace local workers and cause further poverty. What's more, if people are working all the time, they aren't spending money on tourist activities and this is bad for local economies. That's why it's important that voluntourists research their holiday carefully and choose a project that will really benefit the local community.

English Plus Options

CULTURE ■ Punks
I can prepare a quiz about alternative subcultures.

5

An alternative subculture

1 The punk movement started in the USA and the UK in the mid-1970s as a reaction to the political and economic situation at the time. There was a recession and many young people didn't have jobs, so it wasn't surprising that a lot of them became disillusioned with society. This discontent led some young people to rebel against authority. They were concerned with individualism and free thinking and they expressed their ideas and feelings through a new identity, which became known as punk.

2 Punks used their appearance to express their views. They wore clothes that were unconventional and untidy – ripped clothes, T-shirts with anarchic slogans, leather jackets with studs, tight jeans with a lot of zips, and dresses made out of black bin liners. Punks spiked their hair, often into a Mohican style, and used hair dye in bright colours like neon pink, orange and green. Everyday items like chains and padlocks were worn as jewellery. Body piercing was also fashionable, particularly in the eyebrows, nose and lips.

3 Just as punk fashion aimed to shock people, punk music was loud and angry. The records were often produced by the punk bands themselves, not record companies. The lyrics were usually short and direct and they were shouted, not sung. Anything traditional or conventional – popular culture, music, rock groups, the Government, the monarchy – was attacked by punk musicians.

4 In some parts of the world, there are still punks with the same look and ideology as those in the 1970s. However, in Britain and many other countries, punk culture has mixed with mainstream fashion and music. In Britain, the supermodel Agyness Deyn sometimes incorporates elements of punk fashion into her look, and in the USA, there are many pop punk bands such as Green Day. Ironically, this mainstream culture is something that the original punks hated and rebelled against.

1 Check the meaning of the words in the box. Which things can you see in the photos?

> ripped clothes   bin liner   leather jacket
> Mohican   stud   chain   padlock
> safety pin

2 ● 2.34   Match titles a–d with paragraphs 1–4 in the text. Then read, listen and check your answers.

a Current culture   c Sound
b Origin   d Appearance

3 Read the text again and answer the questions.

1 What problems did many young people have in the mid-1970s? Why?
2 How did they react to the situation?
3 Why did punks wear unconventional clothes?
4 What did punks do to their hair?
5 What sort of jewellery did punks wear?
6 Do you think that punk music was relaxing to listen to? Why / Why not?
7 What did punk bands do in their song lyrics?
8 How has punk culture changed since the 1970s?

4 YOUR CULTURE Answer the questions.

1 Was punk culture popular in your country? When?
2 Are there punks in your country today?
3 Do you like modern punk fashion? Why / Why not?
4 What do you think of pop punk music?
5 What other subcultures are popular in your country?

5 TASK Prepare a quiz about alternative subcultures.

1 Work in small groups and choose three or four past and present alternative subcultures, e.g. skinheads, hippies, rockers, goths, etc.
2 Write two quiz questions about each group. You can look at the quizzes in the main units in this book for ideas.
3 Work in small groups and ask and answer your quiz questions.

CULTURE ■ High school elections
I can plan and give an election speech.

1 **Look at the photo below and answer the questions.**

   1 Which country are the people in?

   2 Where do you think the people are?

   3 What do you think is happening?

2 🔊 3.06 **Read and listen to the text. How did Billy become class president?**

3 **Read the text again and answer the questions.**

   1 How can being a class president help you in the future?

   2 What kind of policies do class presidents propose?

   3 What qualities has a good slogan got?

   4 How can supporters help a campaign?

   5 When is a good time to campaign?

   6 What's the most important part of a high school election campaign?

4 **YOUR CULTURE** **Answer the questions.**

   1 Are there class presidents and a student government in your school?

   2 Do you think that it's a good thing to have? Why / Why not?

   3 If you were the class president, what would you campaign for?

   4 Are young people in your country interested in politics?

   5 How do political parties in your country publicize their election campaigns?

5 **TASK** **Prepare and give an election speech.**

   1 Work in small groups. Imagine you are standing for president in the class elections.

   2 Plan two or three policies. Make notes about:
- what you will do
- why these things are important
- how this can be achieved.

   3 Think of a good slogan for your campaign.

   4 Present your speech to the rest of the class.

   5 Have a class vote for the best candidate.

Billy's election blog

Hi! I'm Billy Smith. I go to Ford High School in Virginia, USA, and I'm class president of Class 4, 10th grade. That means that I was elected by my classmates to represent them. As class president, I'm part of the school's student government, and together we're the voice of the students in our school. It's so rewarding to have the opportunity to improve the school, and being class president looks good on college application forms. It makes people realize that you're responsible, hard-working and charismatic. Almost every high school in the country has elections, so what are you waiting for? Read my tips on how to win a high school election and run for class president next year!

If you want to win your high school election, you'll need to ...

★ *plan your policies.*
You should decide what you'll do for the other students if you're elected. For example, you might say that you'll raise money to build a new school library, or try to improve the sports facilities.

★ *think of a good slogan.*
It must be simple, but memorable. If it's funny or it rhymes, great! You want to attract attention and communicate your message at the same time, for example: *Be cool! Improve your school!* or *Vote 'Billy' for a better school!*

★ *publicize your campaign.*
You could make posters and badges with your picture and slogan. Stick the posters in every corridor and classroom, and make your supporters wear your badge.

★ *campaign at all times.*
Talk to students whenever you can, even on the school bus or when you're having lunch. Don't let them leave unless they promise to vote for you!

★ *make a great election speech.*
This is your biggest and most important opportunity to make people vote for you. If your speech is long and boring, people won't listen. You should practise it so you can really connect with the audience.

CULTURE ■ The British sense of humour
I can perform a comedy sketch.

1 Check the meaning of the words and phrases in the box. Then complete the text.

> bizarre   good sense of humour   comedians
> laughter   sarcasm   make fun of

IT'S GOOD TO LAUGH!

Humour is an important aspect of life in Britain. British people can laugh and make jokes in almost any everyday situation. A lot of people consider that a **1**___ is more important in a partner than good looks or money. Britain's comedy industry is huge, with a large number of TV comedy programmes and comedy festivals. The nation's top **2**___ are superstars who perform live shows all over the country in front of thousands of fans. So why are humour and comedy particularly important in Britain? It's well known that **3**___ is good for you. When you laugh, your body releases hormones which make you feel happier, healthier and more optimistic about life. Sunshine has a similar effect, so maybe the British need laughter because the weather is so bad.

Unlike film actors and musicians, Britain's comedians and TV comedy shows generally aren't very popular in other countries. Of course, every nation has its own sense of humour, but the British sense of humour seems to be particularly difficult to understand if you aren't British. The British often use **4**___ – for example, they might say 'Well done!' when someone makes a mistake. British comedy characters are often very unkind and rude to each other and British people love to **5**___ themselves, too. For people from other cultures, this can all seem negative, embarrassing or offensive.

However, not all British humour is incomprehensible to people outside the UK. The Mr Bean TV shows and films, for example, have been popular in over 200 countries over the last twenty years. Mr Bean is funny because he does simple, everyday things in an extremely **6**___, absurd way. People laugh at Mr Bean, but they also appreciate his eccentric behaviour. Loving eccentricity is another important side to the British sense of humour and maybe one that they share with people around the world.

2 ● 3.18   Read and listen to the text. Check your answers to exercise 1.

3 Read the text again and answer the questions.

1 According to the text, what three qualities might be important in choosing a partner?
2 How do people feel when they laugh? Why?
3 What may be the connection with the weather and laughter in Britain?
4 According to the text, what's the difference between British musicians and comedians?
5 Are people in British comedy shows always polite to each other? Explain your answer.
6 Is Mr Bean popular around the world? Explain your answer.
7 According to the text, why do people like Mr Bean?

4 YOUR CULTURE Answer the questions.

1 Is it important to have a good sense of humour in your country?
2 Which are the most popular comedians and TV comedy shows from your country?
3 Is live comedy popular in your country?
4 Do people in your country laugh about the same things as British people?
5 Do you know any British or American TV comedy programmes? Which ones?

5 TASK Prepare and perform a comedy sketch.

1 Work in groups. Plan a short comedy sketch or copy a sketch you have seen on TV. Decide on a role for each person in the group.
2 Write and practise the sketch.
3 Perform the sketch to the class.

CULTURE ■ Boot camps in the USA

I can discuss youth crime and punishment.

8

BOOT CAMPS

The first boot camps were started in the USA in the early 1980s as an alternative to prison for young criminals. The idea was to discipline teenagers with a tough military-style programme. Since then, commercial boot camps have become a popular solution in the USA for dealing with 'problem teenagers'. These special boarding schools have programmes which combine a strict routine with plenty of physical exercise. The focus is on developing the students' self-discipline and self-esteem. By doing challenging outdoor activities and learning new skills, students discover who they are and what they are capable of.

Alvin attended High Winds Academy for two years and the experience changed his life. 'At first, I hated everything – the uniform, getting up early, the strict discipline and all the chores,' said Alvin. 'I wasn't allowed to phone or text my friends back home. And I was very angry with my parents for sending me there.' But gradually, Alvin's attitude changed. As he gained confidence, his school work improved and he became more positive about life. 'I achieved things I never thought I'd be able to do,' he said, 'and I made some great friends.'

Two years ago, Alvin Craig was a very difficult teenager. He was rude and rebellious and was failing at school. 'He argued with us all the time and he missed school a lot,' said Alvin's parents. 'He was out of control and we didn't know how to help him.'

Many teenagers go through a difficult time, but Alvin was heading for serious trouble. 'It was a bad time for me. I was confused and I didn't care about anything,' said Alvin. 'I was hanging around with the wrong people and staying out all night. I couldn't talk to my parents because they didn't seem to understand me.' Alvin's parents were so worried that they decided to send him to a boot camp.

Boot camp may not suit everyone, especially teenagers with serious emotional problems, but for Alvin it worked. Alvin is starting college in September and his parents are very proud of him. 'Our son has completely changed. He's so much happier and he's making plans for the future.'

1 Look at the photo and answer the questions.

1 Where are the people?

2 What are they doing?

3 Why do you think they are doing this?

2 🔊 3.32 Read and listen to the text. What are boot camps? When were they created?

3 Read the text again and answer the questions.

1 Why was Alvin sent to a boot camp?

2 Who was sent to the first boot camps?

3 How do commercial boot camps aim to help students?

4 How long did Alvin spend at a boot camp?

5 How did Alvin feel at first?

6 What is life at a boot camp like?

7 How did Alvin change during his time at boot camp?

4 YOUR CULTURE Answer the questions.

1 Are there boot camps in your country?

2 How do parents and schools deal with teenagers who behave badly?

3 What happens to young people who break the law in your country?

4 What sort of offences and crimes do young people commit?

5 Why do you think young people commit crimes?

6 How do you think young criminals should be treated?

5 TASK Prepare a youth punishment programme.

1 Work in groups. Choose five offences or crimes, for example, playing truant, shoplifting, damaging public property, stealing cars, etc.

2 Discuss and decide what punishments are suitable for each type of offence. Write a sentence to justify each decision.

3 Present your programme to the rest of the class.

4 Have a class debate about the programmes.

Build your vocabulary: adjectives and prepositions

1 Match the sentence halves.

1 We're excited
2 I'm not scared
3 He's happy
4 We're bored
5 I'm good
6 We're polite
7 I was shocked

a with this TV show.
b about his new job.
c by their behaviour.
d about the concert.
e to teachers.
f of spiders.
g at science.

2 Complete the sentences with the prepositions in the box.

about   at   to (x2)   for   ~~of~~   on   with   of

Jen isn't very fond **of** heavy metal.

1 You were very rude ___ your little sister!
2 I'm really worried ___ the exam tomorrow.
3 Are you keen ___ cheese?
4 This car is quite similar ___ ours.
5 My son has just won the competition. I'm so proud ___ him!
6 I'm sorry. Please don't be angry ___ me.
7 Yasmin isn't very good ___ keeping secrets.
8 Hollywood is famous ___ its film industry.

Extend your vocabulary: generations

3 Match the words in the box with the photos.

~~a baby~~   a middle-aged man
an elderly woman   a woman in her twenties
a teenager   a toddler

1 a baby

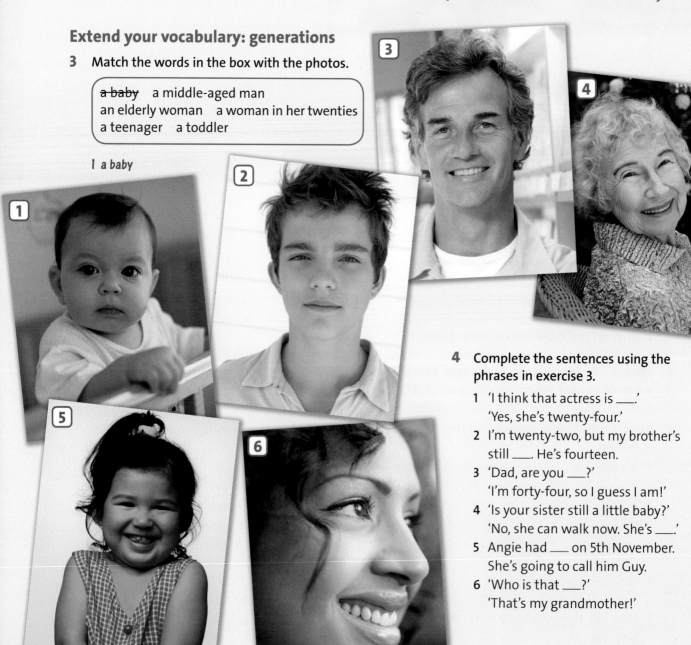

4 Complete the sentences using the phrases in exercise 3.

1 'I think that actress is ___.'
  'Yes, she's twenty-four.'
2 I'm twenty-two, but my brother's still ___. He's fourteen.
3 'Dad, are you ___?'
  'I'm forty-four, so I guess I am!'
4 'Is your sister still a little baby?'
  'No, she can walk now. She's ___.'
5 Angie had ___ on 5th November. She's going to call him Guy.
6 'Who is that ___?'
  'That's my grandmother!'

VOCABULARY BANK ● Verbs and prepositions • Extreme adjectives

Build your vocabulary: verbs and prepositions

1 Choose the correct words.

Is this your bag? No, it doesn't belong for / (to) me.

1 We must concentrate **on** / **at** the lesson. There's a test next week.
2 Did Daniel apologize **for** / **of** eating all your chocolate?
3 I usually prefer coffee **to** / **from** tea.
4 She's very selfish. She doesn't care **to** / **about** other people.
5 When did you get married **to** / **about** Jessica?
6 My friend accused me **at** / **of** cheating in the exam.
7 My mum is going to shout **at** / **to** me! I've lost my coat again.

2 Complete the sentences with the prepositions in the box.

on into from ~~of~~ for (x2) about in

They usually take care **of** their little sister after school. She's nearly five now.

1 Ellen is still searching ___ her mp3 player. She lost it yesterday.
2 Who's going to pay ___ the broken glass?
3 Do you suffer ___ bad headaches? You look awful today.
4 The car crashed ___ a big tree, but all of the passengers survived.
5 I sometimes dream ___ becoming a world-famous scientist.
6 You can't rely ___ Paul. He's always late for everything.
7 Do you believe ___ miracles?

Extend your vocabulary: extreme adjectives

3 Match the words in the box with the photos.

freezing filthy enormous spotless
soaking boiling ~~tiny~~ delicious

1 tiny

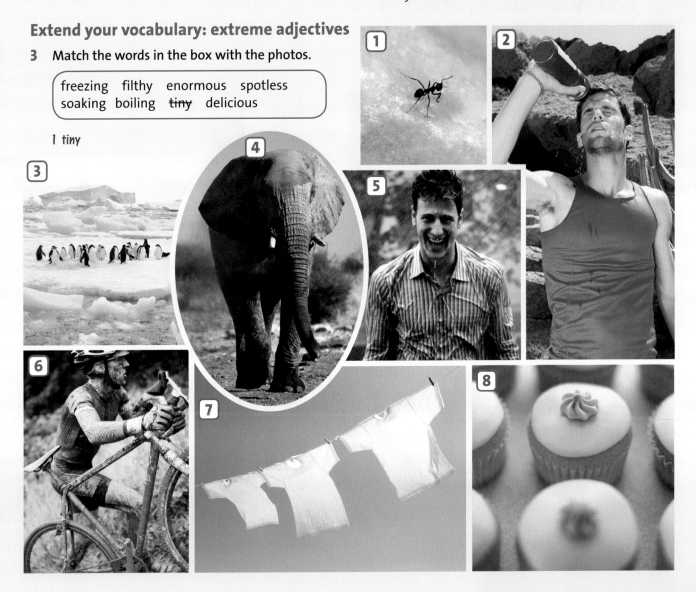

Build your vocabulary: noun suffixes

1 Complete the sentences with nouns formed from the words in brackets. Use the suffixes in the box.

> -ence   -ation   -ment   -ility   -ance   -ion

1 Your health isn't my ___, but you really shouldn't smoke. (responsible)
2 They're testing people's ___. (intelligent)
3 He hasn't been at work for a while now. He's got ___. (depress)
4 He's into alternative medicine. He's tried a lot of different ___. (treat)
5 Do you understand the ___ of these experiments? (important)
6 The doctor gave him a thorough ___ after he fell off the ladder and hit his head. (examine)

2 Complete the sentences using the noun form of the words in the box.

> electric   injure   ⊞   infect   inject
> silent   special

I haven't had a day's **illness** in my life.

1 Leila had a skiing accident and suffered a serious ___.
2 The ___ got better after I'd taken some antibiotics.
3 The nurse gave her another ___ to help with the pain.
4 Could you please be quiet? I need absolute ___ when I'm working.
5 Dr Ranesh is a ___ in cloning.
6 The ___ in the village was cut off because of the storm.

Extend your vocabulary: at the doctor's

3 Look at the photos and read the labels. Then complete the text.

A doctor's surgery

People who are ill should call the doctor's surgery and make an ¹___. They should get to the surgery five minutes before the appointment and tell the ²___ that they've arrived. Then they should sit in the ³___. Their ⁴___ will call them.

The GP may take the ⁵___ temperature or check their blood ⁶___. Sometimes, the GP will ask the ⁷___ to take a blood sample. Often, the GP will give the patient a ⁸___ for some medicine.

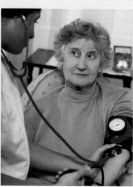

A GP (doctor) checking a patient's blood pressure

A nurse taking a sample of a patient's blood

A prescription

A receptionist making an appointment for a patient

Patients in a waiting room

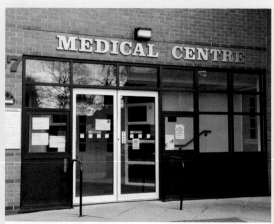

A doctor's surgery

Build your vocabulary: words which are often confused

1 Choose the correct words.

Paul was **bringing** / **carrying** a heavy suitcase.

1 My sister can play the piano well. She's **learning** / **teaching** me how to play it, too.

2 She's very **sensible** / **sensitive**. She always cries when she hears something sad.

3 The sun **rises** / **raises** at about six o'clock now.

4 I'm tired. I had to **pass** / **take** four long exams this week. We'll get the results next month.

5 Aren't you going to put that money in your wallet? You don't want to **loose** / **lose** it.

6 Does Ethan want to sit down and **watch** / **see** TV with us?

7 Captain Magellan led five ships and more than 200 men in the first **travel** / **voyage** around the world.

2 Complete the sentences with one of the words in brackets.

We must show our theatre tickets to that woman. She needs to **check** them. (control / check)

1 Put your mobile phone away. Somebody might ___ it. (steal / rob)

2 These shoes are too small now. They don't ___ me any more. (suit / fit)

3 The bus is here! Please go and ___ Mary. She's over there. (say / tell)

4 'Do you ___ our dog, Scamp?' 'Yes, it was a black Labrador, wasn't it?' (remember / remind)

5 We went on a day ___ to Brighton. (trip / voyage)

6 When did Columbus ___ America? (discover / invent)

7 I've got a problem. Can you give me some ___? (advice / advise)

Extend your vocabulary: methods of transport

3 Match the words in the box with the photos.

| coach van tram ferry lorry minibus scooter ~~helicopter~~ |

1 helicopter

VOCABULARY BANK ■ Negative prefixes • Fashion

5

Build your vocabulary: negative prefixes

1 Complete the sentences. Use the negative prefixes *dis-, il-, im-, in-, ir-, un-*.

She looked **un**happy because some of her answers in the test were incorrect.

1 The number of young people who are ___employed is rising.
2 My great-grandfather couldn't read because he didn't go to school. He was ___literate.
3 I lent you my laptop, but now you've broken it. You're so ___responsible.
4 'The queue in the canteen is really long today. I'm not going to wait' 'Don't be so ___patient!'
5 Copying homework isn't ___legal, but it's ___honest and ___fair.
6 Don't order CDs from that internet company. It's very ___efficient.
7 Sometimes your work is very good and sometimes it isn't. You must try not to be so ___consistent.

Extend your vocabulary: fashion

3 Look at the photos. Complete the labels.

> ~~body~~   combat   designer   diamond
> dyed   high   hooded   leather

1 **body** piercing
2 ___ heels
3 ___ hair
4 ___ top
5 ___ trousers
6 ___ ring
7 ___ jacket
8 ___ sunglasses

2 Complete the sentences using negative prefixes and the adjectives in the box.

> honest   tidy   logical   practical   legible
> ~~organized~~   tolerant

You are late again! Why are you always so **disorganized**?

1 He's ___. He never tells the truth.
2 It's ___ to be afraid of spiders.
3 She always wears ___ clothes. Last week she wore her sandals in the rain!
4 He doesn't like people who are different. He's ___.
5 What's the address on this letter? I can't read it, it's ___.
6 You never pick up the clothes from your bedroom floor. You're really ___.

VOCABULARY BANK ● Prepositions and nouns • Protest

Build your vocabulary: prepositions and nouns

1 Match the sentence halves.

1 Please show your passport on
2 Our neighbours put their house up for
3 I thought the test would be hard, but in
4 I like fruit, for
5 We waited in
6 I deleted your file by

a reality, it was quite easy.
b sale last week.
c line at the check-in.
d arrival at the border.
e mistake. I'm sorry.
f example, apples.

2 Choose the correct words.

On / **In** / **Of** average, there are more women than men in this country.

1 We met my cousins **of** / **on** / **by** chance. We didn't know they'd be there.
2 They went **in** / **of** / **on** holiday to South Africa.
3 You're never **by** / **for** / **on** time. You're always at least five minutes late.
4 I'll lend you my bike, and **for** / **by** / **in** return, can I borrow your mp3 player?
5 Dad had to pay **of** / **in** / **on** cash because he had forgotten his credit card.
6 It's often cheaper if you book the tickets **of** / **in** / **by** advance.

Extend your vocabulary: protest

3 Match the words in the box with 1–8 in the photo.

police   demonstrators   ~~banner~~   placard   flag   high-visibility jacket   helmet   photographer

1 banner

Build your vocabulary: antonyms

1 Match the words in bold with antonyms a–j.

1 The school is very keen on **politeness**.
2 Your bedroom is often **messy**.
3 My aunt wants to **pass** her driving test.
4 Their new dog is **tiny**.
5 There is a lot of **wealth** in London.
6 Our cousins are very **well-behaved**.
7 The latest government policy was a **success**.
8 Be careful. Don't **lose** your wallet.
9 We couldn't find the **exit**.
10 Why are you so **happy**?

a poverty
b find
c enormous
d naughty
e miserable
f fail
g rudeness
h entrance
i failure
j tidy

2 Complete the sentences with antonyms of the words in bold. Use the words in the box.

> ~~adore~~   mean   refuse   innocent   frown
> peace   energetic   rough   rarely   stale

'My parents *adore* opera.' 'My mum and dad **hate** it.'

1 'The sea is **calm** today.' 'That's surprising because it was very ___ yesterday.'
2 'You mustn't ___ in the photo.' 'Don't worry. I'll remember to **smile**.'
3 'Who is **guilty** of the crime in this book?' 'I'm not sure, but the girl is definitely ___.'
4 'This loaf is ___.' 'Don't worry. We've got some **fresh** bread in the cupboard.'
5 'We **frequently** visit the new shopping centre in town.' 'Really? We ___ go there.'
6 'My brother is so ___.' 'My sister is the opposite! She's very **generous**.'
7 'Our grandparents lived in a time of **war**.' 'We're lucky because we live in an age of ___.'
8 'Are you going to **accept** their invitation?' 'I think so. I don't like to ___.'
9 'Is your mum often **tired**?' 'Oh no, she's always ___.'

Extend your vocabulary: expressions with *up* and *down*

3 Match expressions 1–6 with definitions a–f.

1 That American singer is **on the up and up**.
2 I like my aunt. She's very **down-to-earth**.
3 The new school is now **up and running**.
4 That old shop is starting to **go downhill**.
5 My boyfriend and I have had our **ups and downs**.
6 **The downside** of living in a town is the pollution.

a Sensible and practical.
b Becoming more and more successful.
c The negative thing.
d Being used; working.
e Become worse and worse.
f Good times and bad times.

4 Complete the sentences using expressions in exercise 3.

They opened the new shopping centre yesterday. All the shops are *up and running*.

1 I like going to theme parks. But ___ is that they can be expensive.
2 That young footballer is getting better every match. He's really ___.
3 The council should repair our local swimming pool. It's beginning to ___.
4 I can always ask my dad for help with everyday things. He's very ___.
5 Our holiday had its ___. We had some good days and some bad days.

VOCABULARY BANK ■ Collocations with *make* and *do* • Honesty and morals ⑧

Build your vocabulary: collocations with *make* and *do*

1 Complete the sentences with *make* or *do* and the words in the box.

> a complaint   a favour   friends   excuses
> ~~the shopping~~   yoga   decisions

My parents go to the local supermarket to *do the shopping* once a week.

1 He's a politician. He has to ___ difficult ___ all the time.
2 Can you ___ me ___? I need to borrow £5.
3 My mum and my sister like doing exercise. They ___ every weekday evening.
4 That waiter was really rude. I'm going to ___.
5 I'm very shy. It isn't easy for me to ___.
6 You always ___ ! Why don't you just admit it was your fault?

2 Complete the sentences with the correct form of *make* or *do*.

My sister is *doing* a survey about leisure habits.

1 We've ___ some plans for the weekend.
2 It doesn't matter whether you win or lose, just ___ your best.
3 I haven't ___ any phone calls today.
4 Mario always ___ excuses for being late.
5 Shall I buy the red one or the blue one? I like both. I just can't ___ a decision!
6 I've almost finished the housework. I only have to ___ the ironing.

Extend your vocabulary: honesty and morals

3 Complete the sentences with the negative form of the adjectives in brackets.

It was **inconsiderate** to call him at five in the morning! (considerate)

1 Just two of the students were rude, but the teacher gave extra homework to the whole class. It was so ___! (fair)
2 My sister and her boyfriend have separated. She thought he had been ___ to her. (faithful)
3 My uncle never tells the truth. He's completely ___. (moral)
4 It's ___ to ride a bike in the dark without lights. (legal)
5 It's ___ to leave pets alone all the time. (humane)

4 Complete the questionnaire.

A Question of Morals

It's a hot day and a man has left his dog in the car while he's doing the shopping. The windows are open a bit, but it's 37°C outside. That's ___!

ⓐ inhumane   **b** unfaithful

1 Your dad makes three sandwiches for you and your sister. He gives one to you, and two to your sister. That's ___!

a immoral   **b** unfair

2 A man holds open a shop door for an old lady. He's ___!

a considerate   **b** fair

3 Your mum picks you up from school and she's in a hurry to get to the shops. She's driving at 58 km/h but the speed limit is 50 km/h. That's ___!

a immoral   **b** illegal

4 You go to have a shower. Your brother has just used the only two towels and now they're wet. He's so ___!

a inhumane   **b** inconsiderate

5 You've agreed to call on your best friend on Friday evening. Later, another friend invites you to a concert by your favourite band on Friday evening. You say, 'No, thank you. I can't. I'm visiting my best friend.' That's ___!

a faithful   **b** inconsiderate

OXFORD
UNIVERSITY PRESS

Great Clarendon Street, Oxford, OX2 6DP, United Kingdom

Oxford University Press is a department of the University of Oxford.
It furthers the University's objective of excellence in research, scholarship,
and education by publishing worldwide. Oxford is a registered trade
mark of Oxford University Press in the UK and in certain other countries

ISBN: 978 0 19 474859 9

Printed in China

This book is printed on paper from certified and well-managed sources

ACKNOWLEDGEMENTS

The author would like to thank the Oxford University Press teams involved
with English Plus both in Oxford and around the world. I am very grateful not
only for your unerring hard work but also for your friendship and support
throughout this project.

The author would also like to thank (and spend a bit more time with) Mel, Joe
and Sophie.

*The authors and publisher are grateful to those who have given permission to reproduce
the following extracts of copyright material:* p.97 Extract from Oxford Bookworms
Library 6: *Pride and Prejudice* by Jane Austen, retold by Clare West © Oxford
University Press 2008. Reproduced by permission; p.101 Extract from Oxford
Bookworms Library 4: *Gulliver's Travels* by Jonathan Swift, retold by Clare West
© Oxford University Press 2008. Reproduced by permission.

*The publisher and authors would like to thank the following teachers for their contribution
to the development of English Plus:* Romaine Ançay, Ursula Bader, Dominique
Baillifard, Kinga Belley, Jaantje Bodt, Michel Bonvin, Coralie Clerc, Teresita
Curbelo, Yvona Doleželová, Lukas Drbout, Pierre Filliez, Olga Forstová, Christelle
Fraix, Attie van Grieken, Roger Grünblatt, Çağrı Güngörmüş, Christoph
Handschin, Joe Hediger, Jana Vacková Hezinová, Maria Higina, Jaroslava Jůzková;
Martin Kadlec, Urs Kalberer, Lena Kigouk, Joy Kocher, Murat Kotan, Marcela
Kovářová, Jitka Kremínová, Lucie Macháčková, Doubravka Matulová, Jitka
Melounková, Dana Mikešová, Noémi Nikolics, Sabrina Ragno, Denis Richon,
Sonja Rijkse, Susanna Schwab, Dagmar Šimková, Jana Šimková, Nuria Smyth,
Lenka Špačková, Rita Steiner, Anne-Marie Studer, Milan Svoboda, Anneli
Terre-Blanche; Maria Cecilia Verga, Marta Vergara, Donna Van Wely.

*The publisher and authors would like to extend special thanks to Ursula Schaer for sharing
her insights and for her contribution to the course.*

Cover images by: Getty (hikers reading a map/Tyler Stableford/Riser), (sightseeing
at the Louvre/Rayman/Photodisc); iStockphoto (studying on a laptop/
deanm1974); Oxford University Press (teen couple with magazine/Rubberball).

Commissioned photography by: Chris King pp.14, 24, 34, 40, 44, 54, 64, 74, 84.

Illustrations by: David Oakley p.49; ODI pp.68 (brain), 102.

*The Publisher would like to thank the following for their permission to reproduce
photographs and other copyright material:* Alamy Images pp.4 (Jogging on beach/
Olaf Speier), 4 (Teen girl watching television/i love images), 8 (fans), 13,
14 (limousine/Charles Stirling), 17 (1970's Chopper bike/Matthew Richardson),
17 (1970's computer/INTERFOTO), 20, 23, 27 (Yachts racing/Peter Newton),
28 (girl on phone, food), 33 (Cycling accident/Alastair Balderstone), 33 (Crashed
car/Alvey & Towers Picture Library), 38 (elephant, helicopter), 45, 47 (Tourist
guide in Pompeii/Gari Wyn Williams), 47 (Egypt Nile cruise/Rolf Richardson),
48 (Tattoo/Anders Ryman), 52 (label), 54 (Mexican style knitted jacket/Dmitry
Rukhlenko), 54 (Funky leisure shoe/Ian Nolan), 54 (Heart shaped sunglasses/
StockImages), 54 (Apple iPod Nano/D.Hurst), 57 (girls), 58 (protest), 62 (schoolkids,
ballot box), 68 (Sad teenager/Olena Mykhaylova), 70 (coin), 73, 75 (Paralympics
Canada/Megapress), 77 (Wallet with Euro notes/Dave Parker), 77 (Rain on window/
Alan J Jones), 78 (dog), 79, 80 (Minimum wage/vario images GmbH & Co.KG),
81 (text), 83 (Statue of Liberty/Dan O'Flynn), 87 (Dropped five pound note/
Michael Sayles), 87 (Brighton sea front 'no cycling'/Steve Lindridge), 90 (Teenage
girl using mobile phone/CandyBox Photography), 92 (ipod), 98 (Food for a
balanced diet/Valentyn Volkov), 99 (Space Shuttle Discovery lift off/Worldspec/
NASA), 103 (boy), 104 (fans), 107 (Elephant in Thailand/Claudia Wiens),
107 (Charity run school/Paul Springett B), 112 (6), 114 (prescription, medical

centre), 115 (helicopter, bus, van), 117, 119; Arnos Design pp.12 (album),
32 ('What a Waste' poster), 61 (flag), 108 (poster); Aurora Images p.32 (both);
Bridgeman Art Library Ltd p.29 (Surgical operation to amputate a leg (engraving)
(b/w photo), English School, (17th century)/Private Collection); Corbis
pp.4 (Teenage girl shopping/Kevin Dodge), 6 (family), 7 (Arsenal vs. Chelsea/
Rich Eaton/AMA), 8 (couple on beach, babies), 9 (tamagotchi), 10 (Jitterbug
dancing/Underwood & Underwood), 15 (Hippies giving the peace sign/Ocean),
17 (Vintage record player/Lawrence Manning), 22 (Roller coaster/Lester Lefkowitz),
27 (Riding a zip line/Kerrick James), 27 (Mountaineering/John Norris), 29 (baby),
35 (Lab animals/Wolfgang Flamisch), 36 (Medications/Michael Rosenfeld/dpa),
47 (Tourists observing lioness/Herbert Kehrer), 48 (Man with dreadlocks/Ryan
Smith/Somos Images), 48 (Colourful beaded necklaces/Gavin Hellier/JAI),
48 (factory), 51, 52 (cotton), 56 (Model at Eco Chic fashion show/Weda/epa),
62 (better school), 65, 67 (ballot box/Ocean), 72 (Person standing on cliff top/
Martin Sundberg), 72 (Qantas plane in flight/George Hall), 80 (Hairdresser with
unhappy customer/beyond), 82, 88, 90 (Administrator answering phone/Karin
Dreyer/Somos Images), 99 (Model of the completed International Space Station/
Peter Ginter/Science Faction), 99 (space tourist), 100, 113 (all except 2 + 8),
114 (receptionist), 115 (scooter), 116 (shoes, sunglasses); Edbury Press/Arnos
Design p.71 (book); Fairtrade p.52 (logo); Getty Images pp.8 (CND, Marilyn
Monroe), 9 (boots), 11 (club), 12 (George Best, Michael), 22 (Cinema audience/
Jay p. Morgan), 22 (Chopsticks holding sushi/Kick Images/Photodisc), 30 (bee),
38 (beach), 48 (The hand of a Navajo rug weaver/Peter McBride), 48 (Yanomami
Indian girl/Victor Englebert/Time Life Pictures), 48 (dreadlock girl), 62 (money,
football), 67 (protesters/Oli Scarff), 71 (sofa), 87 (Pickpocket/Fredrik Skold),
99 (space station), 109 (speech), 115 (lorry), 116 (Japanese girls, hoodie girl,
dreadlock girl, ring), cover (Hikers reading map/Tyler Stableford/Riser);
iStockphoto pp.19 (Bored boy/Duncan Walker), 22 (Bungee jumping/
VisualCommunications), 28 (crisps), 37 (Lavender flowers and essence/Marilyn
Barbone), 57 (Punk Goth boy/Gail Hardy), 68 (Spanish village), 94 (Spanish
village/Nikada), 106 (Drinks can/Roman Sigaev), 106 (Bag of crisps/winterling),
106 (Hot dog and soda/DNY59), cover (Students with laptop/Dean Mitchell);
Jupiter Images pp.10 (Alice), 58 (flags), 62 (petrol, pool), 85; Kobal Collection
pp.18 (*Pride and Prejudice*), 68 (*Mr Bean*), 97, 110; Lonely Planet/Arnos Design
p.60 (book); Masterfile pp.6 (cinema), 18 (church wedding), 105 (church wedding),
115 (motorbike); MEPL pp.28 (flu), 50 (man), 58 (Gulliver), 101; Motorola
p.9 (phone); Microsoft Games Studio p.62 (game); Oxford University Press
pp.16 (mouse/Photodisc), 18 (Teenage girls/OJO Images), 18 (elephant), 21 (student/
Asia Images RF), 38 (Eiffel Tower/Photodisc), 46 (London/Jan Tadeusz), 57 (Goth/
Gareth Boden), 62 (Autograph signing/image100), 63 (tourists/Image Source),
63 (safari/Image Source), 66 (French flag/EyeWire), 66 (speaker/Comstock),
68 (sign), 69 (Teen boy portrait/Photographer's Choice), 72 (Snake/Photodisc),
72 (Tarantula/Photodisc), 75 (Teen boy/Digital Vision), 76 (learner driver/Dominic
Burke), 78 (coffee shop), 95 (Coffee shop/Image Source), 112 (5, 3, 4, 1, 2), 113 (2),
115 (tram, coach), 115 (Cruise ship/Digital Vision), 118 (children playing sign/
Photodisc), cover (Teen couple with magazine/Rubberball); PA Photos
pp.38 (satellite), 78 (boot camp), 99 (satellite), 111; Photolibrary pp.6 (penguins,
presents), 19 (Young couple holding hands/Corbis), 27 (Whitewater rafting/
Tetra Images), 33 (Kitten on tree branch/Radius Images), 33 (Athlete running in
a triathlon/Corbis), 38 (coach), 44 (balloon), 47 (Surfers on beach/Blend Images),
48 (Punk girl/Blend Images), 48 (Woman with vibrant make up and facial
piercings/Blend Images), 48 (punks, rock band), 58 (Billy Smith), 77 (Bungee
jumping/Andy Belcher), 77 (Friends at a Coming of Age party/Corbis), 80 (iTunes
download/Hermes Images/Tips Italia), 87 (Sports car parked in disabled bay/
Image Source), 91, 92 (band), 108 (punks), 109 (Billy Smith), 113 (8); PR Shots
p.116 (jacket, trousers); Press Association Images pp.67 (Protests outside
Vodafone store/Demotix/Lee Massey), 111 (Thorn Cross 'Boot Camp' style
prison, Warrington/John Giles/PA Archive); PunchStock cover (Young tourists
sightseeing/Photodisc), 6 (boy), 11 (girl); redribbonweek.com p.34 (100% ME
poster); Reuters p.30 (fish therapy); Rex Features pp.8 (Berlin Wall, beehive),
17 (Led Zeppelin/Everett Collection), 31, 34 (boy's poster), 50 (Dietrich),
53 (Jacket worn by Johnny Depp in *Pirates of the Caribbean: The Curse of the Black
Pearl*/Profiles in History/Solent News), 60 (platform, stamps), 67 (Students
demonstrating against higher tuition fees/Sipa Press), 70 (lottery), 78 (results),
104 (Twiggy/Zdenko Hirschler), 114 (blood test, blood pressure, waiting room);
Ian Robinson p.105 (Old Trafford); Science Photo Library pp.15 (moon),
28 (blood test), 29 (nanobots), 34 (lungs); Sony p.9 (Walkman); Chris Stocker
p.42; Superstock p.39; Topfoto p.12 (Maxine); UKYP p.58 (teens), 93.